GUIDEPOSTS

Everyday Miracles

Everyday Miracles

Realizing God's Presence
in Ordinary Life

MARJORIE L. KIMBROUGH

CARMEL, NEW YORK 10512

www.guidepostsbooks.com

This Guideposts edition is published by special arrangement with Abingdon Press.

Copyright © 1997 by Dimensions for Living

Library of Congress Cataloging-in-Publication Data

Kimbrough, Marjorie L., 1937-
  Everyday miracles : realizing God's presence in ordinary life / Marjorie L. Kimbrough.
    p.   cm.
  ISBN 0-687-05147-9 (hc : alk. paper)
  1. Miracles.   2. Christian life—Anecdotes.   I. Title.
BT97.2.K47   1997
231.7'3—dc21   97-25806
                                                                                         CIP

Scripture quotations, unless otherwised noted, are from the New Revised Standard Version Bible. Copyright © 1989 by the Division of Christian Education of the National Council of the Churches of Christ in the United States of America.

Scripture quotations marked TLB are from *The Living Bible*, copyright © 1971. Used by permission of Tyndale House Publishers, Inc., Wheaton, Il. 60189. All rights reserved.

www.guidepostsbooks.com
Jacket and interior design by José R. Fonfrias
Jacket photo copyright © Valder/Tormey/International Stock
Typeset by Composition Technologies, Inc.

MANUFACTURED IN THE UNITED STATES OF AMERICA

For my sister, Lucy, whose very life is a miracle
Praise God!

Contents

Miraculous Prayers 24

The Miracle of Prayer ∾ The Miracle of Forwarding Mail ∾ The Miracle of Fasting ∾ The Miracle of Repair ∾ The Miracle of Peace ∾ The Miracle of Revival ∾ The Miracle of Coupons ∾ The Miracle of Salvation ∾ The Miracle of Surrender ∾ The Miracle of Independence ∾ The Miracle of Intercession ∾ The Miracle of Certification ∾ The Miracle of the Dent ∾ The Miracle of Sixty-five Feet ∾ The Miracle of Prayers with Legs ∾ The Miracle of a Home ∾ The Miracle of the List ∾ The Miracle of Blinking ∾ The Miracle of Second Birth

Miraculous Blessings 47

The Miracle of the Gift ∾ The Miracle of Wedding Finances ∾ The Miracle of Timing ∾ The Miracle of New Shoes ∾ The Miracle of Graduation ∾ The Miracle of Opportunity ∾ The Miracle of Water ∾ The Miracle of Monetary Assistance ∾ The Miracle Fall ∾ The Miracle of Walking ∾ The Miracle of Help ∾ The Miracle of Disability ∾ The Miracle of Organ Donation ∾ The Miracle Shooting

Miraculous Encounters 63

The Miracle of Witness ∾ The Miracle of the Back Page ∾ The Miracle of Hesitation ∾ The Miracle of Work ∾ The Miracle of Generosity ∾

Miraculous Healings   83

Miraculous Rescues   109

Contents

Miraculous Faith 152

~ *Introduction* ~

WHAT IS A MIRACLE? Must it be a mysterious, mighty, unexplainable act of an unseen power or force in the universe? Is it the direct intervention of God in the lives of His children at a critical time of need? Is a miracle a simple unexpected and unexplainable blessing in the life of an ordinary person? Do miracles only happen to God's chosen people—past or present? Must there be an act of nature, a parting of the waters, or could there simply be a neighbor bringing a glass of water when one's own supply has been disconnected?

In my estimation, a miracle is any and all of these things. There are wondrous miracles and there are ordinary miracles. God is sovereign and can effect all of these miracles in either spectacular or mundane manners. God does whatever He wants to, whenever and however He chooses.

I believe miracles happen every day to ordinary people. They are God's unique way of intervening in our lives. Some of us do not recognize our everyday miracles, and as a result, we miss the opportunity to strengthen our belief in God and our opportunities to serve and witness as we work to realize His kingdom on earth. We do not have to be especially gifted or spiritual to experience a miracle, but we will become both gifted and spiritual if we expect and recognize miracles as they occur in our lives and in the lives of those around us.

Whenever we are blessed in ways that seem to us to be extraordinary; whenever we feel the power of God moving in our lives, protecting us from harm; whenever we escape death in ways that mere mortals and medical technology cannot explain, we have experienced a miracle. While collecting the meditative stories that appear in this book, I decided that anything the interviewee considered to be a miracle was, in fact, a miracle. If the event changed their lives or strengthened their faith, I believe that they benefited from their personal act of God, their miracle.

Peter Wagner defines the gift of miracles as "the special ability that God gives to certain members of the Body of Christ to serve as human intermediaries through whom it pleases God to perform powerful acts that are perceived by observers to have altered the ordinary course of nature" (Peter Wagner, *Your Spiritual Gifts Can Help Your Church Grow* [Ventura: Regal Books, 1985], p. 237). Mr. Wagner implies that only selected Christians have the gift of miracles. Yet I believe that anyone can have that gift and be that intermediary that God selects.

In some of the stories that follow, you will meet some of God's intermediaries. Most of them did not know about the gift of miracles; they just did what they felt led to do. As a result, they experienced what they considered to be a miracle. I agree that they did in fact experience a miracle because I believe that God leads whom He will when He will, and the result is always miraculous.

We must recognize and expect miracles to happen every day. Jesus set the example; He expected miracles. He told His disciples, "Cure the sick, raise the dead, cleanse the lepers, cast out demons" (Matthew 10:8). He did not instruct His disciples to get special training; in fact, He told them that all they needed was faith. His charge to all of us was, "Have faith in God. Truly I tell you, if you say to this mountain, 'Be taken up and thrown into the sea,' and if you do not doubt in your heart, but believe that what you say will come to pass, it will be done for you. So I tell you, whatever you ask for in prayer, believe that you have received it, and it will be yours" (Mark 11:22-24). When Jesus cast out demons that the disciples had failed to cast out, He told them, "This kind can come out only through prayer" (Mark 9:29).

Asking in faith serves as a miracle agent. Some of the people in the following stories asked in faith, and they received. They expected a miracle. They did what Jesus advised, and they were blessed, saved, rescued, revived, empowered, and energized to witness for a God Who is all powerful. Praise God!

Miracles happen every day. Expect yours!

Everyday Miracles

Miraculous Voices

The Miracle of Redirection

IT WAS EARLY EVENING on October 17, 1989, and Lucy was on her way home from her teaching assignment in Alameda, California. She normally took the Nimitz Freeway to her home in El Cerrito, but as she approached the freeway entrance, "something" told her to use the side streets. Turning onto the side street she felt her car shake violently. Believing that she had a flat tire, Lucy got out of her car to investigate. To her surprise several other motorists were doing the same thing. Then there was a loud noise as the freeway collapsed, killing forty-two persons and trapping many more. The shaking Lucy had experienced was not a flat tire but an earthquake having a magnitude of 7.1. The resulting shock had caused the collapse of the two-level interstate freeway on which she normally traveled every evening. While watching the freeway she had almost entered go down, Lucy realized that she had experienced the miracle of redirection.

Perhaps that "something" that told her to use the side streets was an angel, her guardian angel, and having obeyed its redirection, she was saved.

What about those who were trapped and killed? Had their guardian angels also redirected them? Had they been too stubborn, too busy, or too unbelieving to listen? Did they miss their miracles? How many of us miss our miracles by ignoring those inner voices that warn us that what we have planned is not the best for us? Are we listening, watching, and waiting for direction and/or redirection? Or are we insisting on having our own way, proceeding with what we had planned? I wonder.

Miracles happen every day. Expect yours!

Lord, help me to listen to the inner voice that directs and redirects me today. Amen.

The Miracle of Recognition

JOHNNY MILLS AWOKE IN A HOSPITAL. He had been drugged and sexually abused. He did not know who he was or where he was. He only knew that he was hurting. The doctors and nurses kept asking him to tell them his name, but he could not remember it. There was a woman with them who seemed strangely familiar, but he could not remember who she was either. Finally he heard the doctor tell the woman that if he could not remember his name, they would have to institutionalize him. He did not know who he was, but he knew that he did not want to be institutionalized.

Although he did not know it at the time, the woman with them was his mother. She looked at him with love and said in a voice that he recognized, "Johnny, tell them your name." Hearing his name in that familiar voice that he had known since birth unlocked his mind. He responded automatically: "My name is Johnny Mills." The doctors had not intended for his mother to prompt him by saying his name, but she believed in the miracle of recognition, and it brought her son back to her.

Johnny is still in recovery. He was drugged and abused by a person he believed to be a family friend. Because of his experience, Johnny harbors some feelings of guilt. But Johnny knows that his mother loves him and will do all that she can to help make him whole. He recognizes her love even as he recognized her voice calling his name. It was a miracle!

Miracles happen every day. Expect yours!

Lord, help us to recognize those around us who are sick and abusive so that we may keep our children safe. Amen.

The Miracle of the Burning House

IT HAD BEEN JUST SIX MONTHS since Dawn's father had died. He had suffered a massive heart attack while he was playing with her. Although she was a teenager, her father often played with her, roughhousing and teasing her. But that last time had been too much. He was dead.

As she studied in his office, she felt strangely close to him. She had washed her gym clothes and decided to lay them across a space heater to dry. She fell asleep, and while she was sleeping, the house caught on fire. Dawn's mother and brother both had smelled smoke and had retreated to safety. They stood outside the house and wondered where Dawn was. Dawn was still asleep.

As she comfortably slept with her father's books and papers around her,

Dawn started to dream. She dreamed that she could see her father playing with her; she even heard his voice softly calling to her. Then the voice grew louder. Dawn could hear her father calling, telling her to wake up. In trying to answer him, she awoke. Smoke surrounded her. She realized that the house was on fire, and she crawled to the door. Fortunately, the office door led directly outside.

Dawn found her mother and brother outside praying for her and praising God for her safe delivery. When she told them that her father had awakened her, her mother accepted what she said to be a miracle. Miraculously, the father who had loved her had saved her.

Isn't God just like that? The Father who loves us saves us.

Miracles happen every day. Expect yours!

Lord, thank You for the miracle of salvation. Amen.

The Miracle of Exposure

HENRY WAS BLESSED with a wonderful tenor voice. He had won the title of most outstanding gospel soloist and directed the gospel choir in his church. Prior to entering college, his musical exposure had been limited to gospel and popular selections. One semester he enrolled in a voice class, and the instructor not only noticed his wonderful voice but also felt that he had real potential for performing classical selections. Until that class, Henry had not been exposed to classical music.

The instructor talked with him, encouraged him, and discussed the possibility of his majoring in music. But Henry was a single parent and had some difficulty financing his education. For a brief period he dropped out of school; when he returned, he again enrolled in voice class. This time the instructor assigned him an aria to learn. He was given a tape of the aria being performed in Italian by the famous Pavarotti, and he was told to do the best he could. Henry mastered the notes, phrasing, and musical expression and was ready to work with the instructor in short order. He was more excited than he had ever been, and he made the decision to major in music. How wonderful it was for him to have been exposed to classical music.

Henry performed that aria, "M'appari Tutt Amor," from the opera *Martha* by Friedrich von Flotow for the college choir's spring concert, and he received a standing ovation. It was a miracle, a miracle of exposure!

Miracles happen every day. Expect yours!

Lord, expand our horizons and make us receptive to new forms of worship and service. We often limit ourselves to one form of response to all that You have provided. We thank You for the many ways of lifting up our voices to You. Amen.

The Miracle of Insight

WHEN DIANNE FEINSTEIN WAS MAYOR of San Francisco, she had tremendous insight into the potential problems that would be faced in the event of an earthquake. She knew that many areas needed to be upgraded or retrofitted to withstand a natural disaster of the type possible in the San Francisco area. She pleaded with the city leaders, who did not have the same insight, but they failed to approve the proposed enhancements. They told her that the city could not afford it.

But something would not allow the mayor to go along with her defeat. She rallied to overrule the city leaders and embarked upon the retrofitting or upgrading of such city landmarks as Candlestick Park.

On October 17, 1989, during the playing of the World Series in Candlestick Park, a powerful earthquake struck. More than fifty-six thousand people were present in the ballpark when the quake occurred, and all escaped injury. The recently refurbished park had held during the tremor. It was a miracle, a miracle of insight.

How many times do we fail to listen to the voices that beg us to take care of potential problems? How many times could disaster be avoided if we only had the insight to act as Dianne did? With God's help, tragedy was averted and a miracle was enacted.

Miracles happen every day. Expect yours!

Lord, teach us to use our insight and to be constant in prayer so that we will not miss either our blessings or our miracles. Amen.

The Miracle of Shared Time

EVEN AS A LITTLE GIRL, Yunice had shared time with her grandmother. That time was always special, and Yunice enjoyed her frequent visits. But as Yunice grew up, her teenage life was so busy with school and church activities that visiting was no longer a priority. Somehow Yunice felt that she could always visit her grandmother later.

When Yunice enrolled in college, there were greater demands on her time, and she knew that she would not be visiting her grandmother very often. Then she heard a little voice that said, "Your grandmother will not always be with you; make time for her now." Yunice carefully considered her spring class schedule and decided to spend her three-hour break between classes with her grandmother. During those visits her grandmother motivated her, shared stories from the past with her, and offered advice for the future.

When Mother's Day came that spring, all of Yunice's family gathered at her grandmother's house. After food and fellowship, her grandmother kissed Yunice good-bye. Yunice was touched by the kiss and thought about it as she drove home. Two days later, her grandmother died. Yunice remembered that kiss, but most of all she remembered the time shared and the little voice that had told her that she would not always have her grandmother with her.

Yunice defines a miracle as an event in the physical world that surpasses all known human or natural powers and is ascribed to a divine or supernatural cause. She says that little voice was a divine voice that spoke to her, and she is glad she listened.

Miracles happen every day. Expect yours!

Lord, thank You for grandparents and for the time that we share with them. Amen.

The Miracle of Mama's Voice

CARMEN HAD JUST GOTTEN OFF FROM WORK. She was tired and sleepy as she worked the night shift; her "day" had been especially long. She was hopeful that she would make it home without falling asleep behind the wheel of her car. But she was just too sleepy, and she kept dozing. Each time she snapped out of her doze, she wondered how many seconds she had been asleep. She knew that it would only take one second of semiconsciousness to have an accident. Even knowing all of this, she dozed one more time, falling into a deep sleep.

Carmen is not sure how long she slept, but she does remember dreaming. She dreamed of her mother who had been dead for several years. Her mother seemed to be warning her about something, and she very clearly heard her mother's voice yell, "STOP!" Carmen woke up immediately, slamming on the brakes. She barely missed colliding with a tractor trailer truck that passed right in front of her! This near-disaster woke Carmen up, and she made it home without further incident.

As she later reflected, she realized that although she had not heard her mother's voice in many years, it was easily recognizable. She knew that just hearing that voice would have awakened her, but the order to stop provided the urgency needed. It had to be a miracle, for there was no doubt in her mind that her mother's voice had saved her. She sometimes has trouble recalling her mother's face, but she could never forget that voice of comfort and love that still was so familiar. On that particular night, Mama's voice had been a saving miracle.

Miracles happen every day. Expect yours!

Lord, teach us to rest before driving, so that we are not always counting on Your miracles to save us. But thank You for saving us in spite of ourselves. Amen.

The Miracle of the Silent Bell

DEBBIE IS A REGISTERED NURSE, and sometimes she hears God speaking to her through inner voices and silent bells. She can not explain what happens; it is simply that when there is a need around her, she hears it calling out to her, and she responds.

While she was on duty one night, she seemed to hear a silent bell. She knew that all of her patients had call bells; and, although none of them was ringing or lighted, she knew that there was a need. A patient who was scheduled to be discharged the next day appeared to her to be the focus of that need. Although it was not time to make her regular rounds, Debbie rushed to that patient's room. She found her patient clutching her chest and having difficulty breathing. It was a heart attack, and the patient very nearly lost her life.

Even as Debbie was responding to the crisis, she wondered why the patient had not used her call bell. Then she noticed that the call bell had fallen to the floor out of the patient's reach. But, miraculously, Debbie had heard that silent bell, and she was glad that she had responded to that silent yet persistent ringing. It had saved her patient's life.

Miracles happen every day. Expect yours!

Lord, make us aware of those inner voices and silent bells that alert us to danger and call us to action in Your name. Amen.

The Miracle Voices

EVEN AS A LITTLE GIRL, Nicole used to hear voices. She would hear her name being called, and she would answer only to discover that no one was there. Sometimes her mother would enter the room, finding Nicole alone, and would ask who she was talking to. Somewhat frustrated, Nicole would say, "You just called me."

As Nicole grew older, she no longer heard the voices. She was quite relieved, for she had begun to think that something was wrong with her. But then, one day the voices returned, and they miraculously saved her life.

At the time, Nicole was a high school student. She and her mother had been out to dinner and were walking home. Nicole walked ahead of her mother, intending to have the apartment door opened by the time her mother arrived. It was a rainy evening, and it was just getting dark, so Nicole was hurrying. As she approached the end of the block, she heard her name being called. She remembered the voices from her past and did not want to respond. But there was an urgency in the voice, and she was sure that it was her mother. Nicole stopped and turned around to answer. Just then a tree that was a few feet in front of her snapped and broke, covering the sidewalk in her path.

A pedestrian rushed to her aid and commented that it was a good thing that she had stopped in time. Nicole turned to her mother, who had also rushed up, and said, "It was a good thing that you called me." Her mother responded, "I did not call you. It must have been one of those miracle voices."

Nicole is now in college, and she still wonders about the voices. She feels certain that she would have been crushed had she not heard the voice and stopped. She does not know whether she has a guardian angel or whether she has good instincts, but she does know that a miracle saved her.

Miracles happen every day. Expect yours!

Lord, Samuel heard his name being called, and he responded as Your servant. Help us to respond to Your call. Amen.

The Miracle of Divine Shaking

MYRTICE SAYS THAT ON OCTOBER 4, 1995, the Lord started getting her ready for her miracle. She went to midday Bible study at church and returned home to enter into fervent prayers while kneeling by her bed. Her constant thought was, "Lord, what do You want me to pray for?" Not receiving an answer, she just prayed that the Lord would bless and protect her from harm and danger.

That night Myrtice, who is eighty years old and nearly blind, drifted off to sleep. The wind was blowing, and a light rain was falling; she slept lightly, waking up twice. The third time she dozed off, she fell into a deep sleep. She no longer heard the storm that had been called Hurricane Opal. Suddenly Myrtice felt herself being severely shaken. She knew that no hand was on her, but she felt powerful shaking. She was awakened, and she heard a cracking noise outside her window. Then she heard a voice that told her to go to her basement. She immediately obeyed, and as soon as she reached the basement steps, there was a tremendous crash. The oak tree outside her bedroom window had fallen onto her house, destroying her bedroom, the guest bedroom, the living room, and the dining room. Myrtice knew that God had miraculously shaken her awake. If she had remained in her bed, the tree would have fallen directly in her path.

Myrtice says that her constant prayer had been, "Take care of me, Lord." She knows that He did, for although much of her house was destroyed, she still lives and can witness to the saving power of the Lord.

Miracles happen every day. Expect yours!

Lord, teach us to be obedient in prayer and to remember the great blessings we enjoy every day. Amen.

Miraculous Visions

The Miracle of Life

INA GAMBLE WAS PREGNANT. It was a new marriage and a new baby, and she was ecstatic. The feel of new life developing in one's body is truly a miracle, and Tina praised God for it. I observed the beauty and serenity that seemed to emanate from her as her pregnancy progressed.

The time came for her to be delivered, and her husband and family waited at the hospital for the news of the birth. The baby was born; he was a beautiful boy. Immediately after his birth Tina started hemorrhaging uncontrollably. She was losing blood by the pint, and the doctors feared that they had lost her. She was not breathing.

Tina lived to tell what happened during that brief period in which she ceased to breathe. She says that she was headed down a long tunnel. At the end of the tunnel was a bright light. She was drifting toward the light. She felt an incredible sense of peace, for she knew that Jesus was in the light.

When she got to the end of the tunnel, she looked around, but she did not see Jesus. She knew she had to return because Jesus was not there.

The doctors said that her experience was not unusual, for others who have survived tell similar stories. However, while Tina was on her journey in the tunnel, her family was on their knees praying for her and for the baby. They knew that both they and that angelic baby needed her. That baby was appropriately named Gideon, the mighty warrior and deliverer.

Miracles happen every day. Expect yours!

Lord, we are so grateful for life through birth and through rebirth. Amen.

The Miracle of Observation

GENEVA WORKED IN A HOSPITAL AS AN AIDE. She often had to record and observe body fluids eliminated by patients. In her observations, she noticed that the patient fluids had a very different look from her own. She knew that the doctors did not seem to think there was anything abnormal about the patients' fluids, so she thought there must be something abnormal about her own.

Then Geneva really got serious about the observation of her own body. She noticed significant weight gain. At one point there was so much swelling in her legs that she was unable to bend them, making it impossible to walk. After several visits to the doctor, she was informed that she was losing protein and needed rest and medication. She was led to believe that she would be ill for quite some time, rest was essential, eventually the swelling would subside, and walking would be easier. The doctor told her that she was very fortunate to have observed the differences in her bodily functions.

Geneva could not accept the doctor's advice. She needed to go to work; she did not have time to rest. She believed that God could and would heal her. Being unable to sleep, she sat in her hallway reading her Bible. Suddenly the hallway became cloudy. It seemed as if there was a white smoke or fog covering everything. The fog moved over her, and she could feel the swelling leaving her legs. She knew that she was being healed. She became very sleepy and dozed right where she sat. When she awoke, the fog was gone and her legs were normal.

Geneva went to the doctor the next day, and he could not believe the change in her condition. He ordered tests, which revealed the fact that healing had taken place. Although the doctor was reluctant to call the healing a miracle, Geneva was not. She knew that her own observations of her bodily functions had led to a diagnosis, and her God had sent a miraculous cloud of healing. She had observed that too!

Miracles happen every day. Expect yours!

Lord, make us more observant of the world around us. Where there is sickness, poverty, and distress, make us responsive as Your servants. Amen.

The Miracle of the Dream

MELANIE BELIEVES THAT GOD reveals things to her in dreams. She always knows when God is speaking to her, and she responds.

One night Melanie awoke suddenly; she could not go back to sleep, and although it was 2:00 A.M., she dressed and went to her parents' house. Her mother was shocked to see her at the door at such an early hour, but she knew that something very important had happened.

Melanie told her mother that she had dreamed that her father had died. She told her mother that they had to get him to the hospital immediately or he would die. Melanie's mother did not believe her. She only said, "Your father has been tired, but he is not ill. I am sure that your dream has some other meaning." But Melanie insisted. She reminded her mother of her past correct predictions. Her mother finally agreed to take her father to the doctor the next day. But Melanie begged her to take him right then. She said, "Tomorrow may be too late."

Her mother finally agreed, and they awakened her father and told him what Melanie had said. Being a believer that God does speak to us in dreams, he went to the hospital.

All they could tell the emergency room doctor was that the father had been complaining of tiredness, and they wanted him to be given a thorough examination. Of course the doctor advised them that the situation did not seem to be an emergency and they could make an appointment the next day. But because the two women, especially Melanie, were so insistent, the doctor agreed to examine the father.

In relatively short order it was determined that the father had walking pneumonia. Without immediate attention, he would have died within two weeks.

Melanie knew that God had spoken to her, and she saved her father's life. It was a miracle.

Miracles happen every day. Expect yours!

Lord, teach us to listen to the many ways You speak to us. Some of us see visions; some of us have dreams; and some of us hear voices, but all of us can hear You if we listen. Amen.

The Miracle of Choice

QUIANA'S FRIEND MADE A CHOICE that saved her life, and to all who were aware of the situation, it was a miraculous choice. Quiana told me that her friend was severely allergic to bees. She even had to carry a special medicine kit around with her during the spring and summer months. A sting could result in death.

One summer day this friend was driving along with her twelve-year-old daughter. Her daughter opened the window, and a bee flew in and stung the mother. Although the mother was able to pull off the road and stop the car, she passed out. Her daughter called 911 for help, and her unconscious mother was soon transported to the hospital.

The doctors were not hopeful. The allergic reaction had resulted in the type of swelling that usually meant death. Quiana and her family joined the daughter in prayer for the mother. The mother survived, but had an interesting story to tell about her hours of unconsciousness.

The mother says that she had an out-of-body experience. She saw a bright light. She was in a tunnel, rapidly traveling to the light. At one end of the tunnel, she clearly saw her deceased grandmother, and at the other end of the tunnel her children were waiting. (Her youngest child was only two years old, and it was the child's crying and reaching that made a special impression on the mother.) Although the light was appealing, she felt that she just could not travel toward it. She is convinced that she purposefully made a choice to travel toward her children. Shortly after she made that choice, she regained consciousness.

The doctors all felt that she was near death, but they noticed the sudden improvement in her condition, and they said that it appeared that she chose not to die. It was a miraculous choice.

Miracles happen every day. Expect yours!

Lord, thank You for the choices that we make to live our lives in service to You through those who need us most. Amen.

The Miracle of Visualization

AT THE AGE OF THIRTY-SEVEN, Marlene, mother of four, was diagnosed with aggressive skin cancer. The doctor told her that she had a malignant melanoma that would require several operations. Marlene took leave of her job as a financial consultant and had the operations.

After the surgeries, the doctor told her that her cancer was terminal. She was encouraged to undergo chemotherapy and other experimental treatments, but she refused. She was given less than a year to live.

But Marlene believes in miracles, and she began an aggressive program of meditation, prayer, yoga, and visualization. Visualization is an often overlooked form of treatment. Many of us fail to realize that we may have to visualize ourselves being cured or actually experiencing the miracle before it occurs. Rather than saying that we'll believe it when we see it, it may be more appropriate to say that when we believe it, we will see it.

Marlene started seeing little "Pac-man"-like figures running through her body, gobbling up the cancer. The Pac-man figures were being driven by meditation, prayer, and yoga, and they were effecting her miracle.

Today, Marlene has survived her cancer more than nine years. The doctor who first issued the bleak diagnosis says that her survival is truly a miracle.

Miracles happen every day. Expect yours!

Lord, teach us to believe in miracles and to visualize their actualization in our lives. Amen.

The Miracle of Guardianship

HER NAME IS JOSEPHINE, and she has been the legal guardian of more than twenty children. Because she believes so firmly in a good, solid education, she sacrifices having a phone so that her children can attend private school.

Josephine works as an assistant pastor at her neighborhood church. Her biological children fell victim to the streets of Chicago, and Josephine is determined not to let other children be lost. She preaches a gospel of love and forgiveness. She tries to keep her foster children out of the environment that leads to crime. Sadly, that environment is often the public school. So, Josephine uses every penny she makes to pay the private-school tuition, even those pennies that are needed to pay the phone bill. She says that she can survive without a phone, but her children cannot survive without a good education.

But Josephine does not do it all alone. All of her children work. They have after school jobs or before school jobs, and they have learned to appreciate the sacrifices that Josephine makes for them. All of the children are well-behaved, and they know what their success means to their mother.

Josephine's walls are decorated with plaques that she and the children have earned. They are proud, and they want their mother to be proud of them. They realize that having a guardian is a miracle. They know that many other children just like them have no one to look out for them and to care about them.

Josephine cares enough to sacrifice her phone. What will I sacrifice? Her story is a miracle of guardianship.

Miracles happen every day. Expect yours!

Lord, make us aware of those children around us who need someone to care. Amen.

The Miracle House

DURING THE SUMMER OF 1995, Carol began to wonder where she would live when she returned to college in the fall. Her attempts to secure campus housing had failed, but she was certain that God would provide. Although her mother was reluctant to allow her daughter to return to the campus without an address, Carol let her know that God had shown her the exact location and description of the house in which she would reside during the fall. Because Carol's mother is a deeply religious person, she believed in her daughter's vision.

Carol actually had had several visions. Each vision had given more detail, and Carol knew exactly what God had planned. Carol was directed to travel west on Cascade Road in Atlanta. She was to turn left at the third light after she had passed Interstate 285. That street would lead her directly to the house. She knew that she would recognize the house, for she had seen it clearly in her vision. It was a brick house with a two-car garage on the right and a swimming pool and patio on the left. The house would contain four bedrooms and two and a half bathrooms. Carol also knew that two women would reside in the house, and she would be employed to care for one of them in exchange for room and board.

Athough Carol was able to follow her directions and go to the house, which she recognized immediately, she did not feel comfortable just showing up at the doorstep, saying that she had been sent by God. So she went to her major department at the college and told her department chair that she needed housing. He told her that a friend had just called requesting a student who, after classes, might be willing to care for her elderly mother in exchange for room and board. Although Carol was given directions to the house, she did not need them. It was the house she had seen in her visions.

Carol moved into her miracle house within two days.

Miracles happen every day. Expect yours!

Lord, thank You for providing for our daily needs. Teach us not to be faithless but believing. Amen.

The Miracle of the Nonexistent Beacon

EDWARD, AN AIR FORCE CAPTAIN, announced to his flight crew that they had an assignment. They were to fly to Sacramento to pick up some vitally needed equipment for a downed aircraft. The crew of six departed late that night.

An hour after takeoff, the left engine of their plane heated rapidly and then exploded. Edward managed to maintain control by increasing power on the remaining engine; however, it was virtually impossible to maintain the current altitude with one engine.

Within minutes, the second engine exploded. Edward remembers being ejected from the aircraft as it seemed to disintegrate beneath him. Knowing that he was about to die, Edward remembers giving thanks to God for his personal salvation through Jesus Christ. Praying as he sailed through the air, Edward tried to pull the rip-cord of his parachute. He could not do it because his wrist was broken, but miraculously the parachute opened.

He hit the ground hard, fracturing his leg, back, and skull. Again, miraculously, he did not lose consciousness, and he began to crawl free of his parachute and away from the forest fire started by the crash. He called out to his crew, but there was no answer. He knew he had to remain calm, trust in God's continued deliverance, and move away from the flames that were rapidly approaching.

He looked away from the flames and saw a solitary bright light, which he assumed to be a beacon. He did not understand why the beacon was not revolving, but he was so grateful for its light. With the light to guide him, Edward made it down a slippery slope into a cold mountain stream. Again, miraculously, his landing in the stream kept down the swelling of his broken limbs and provided safety from the fire.

Edward stayed in and near the stream the rest of the night. He was in indescribable pain, but his prayers and thoughts that God had spared him helped him endure the night.

In the morning he was able to gather a stick to help him walk and a log to help him float downstream. He ended up at the ranch of William Randolph Hearst. The caretaker rescued him and asked if he had been helping to fight the fire. Edward explained that he had been in the plane crash, but the caretaker informed him that everyone on the plane had been accounted for and was dead.

Then Edward remembered that a sailor who had missed his ship had asked for a ride. Edward had refused him because regulations permitted only crew members on his assignment. One of the crew members had allowed that sailor to stow away, and his body had been identified as Edward's.

The caretaker made the necessary phone calls, and Edward was taken to the hospital for a six-month stay. The Air Force investigation team could not believe that Edward had found his way to the stream down a steep slope in total darkness. Edward told them of the beacon that guided him. But they informed him that they had searched the area and there was no beacon or light of any kind within fifty miles. It was a miracle.

Miracles happen every day. Expect yours!

Lord, thank You for sending lights to guide us in darkness. Amen.

Miraculous Prayers

The Miracle of Prayer

UNT SUE LIVED IN HAYS, KANSAS. She was a very religious person who prayed as she planted corn and worked in the fields of the small farm that supported her. Although she lived alone, she was often visited by relatives and friends. Her many nieces and nephews loved to help Aunt Sue pick corn.

It was during one of the many visits of the children that a severe tornado struck. The children were in the fields with Aunt Sue, and they knew that there was a safe place below ground where they could go for refuge. But Aunt Sue forbade it. She told the children to gather around her on their knees and join with her in prayer. The children were frightened but obedient.

As the storm gained in momentum, the children listened intently to Aunt Sue's prayer. John was among those children, and he says that her prayer was something like this, "Lord, You know that I am a poor widow woman, and I need this farm to live. I have worked too long and too hard to lose it all now.

Please don't let this storm take my farm. Build a fence all around me and these children, and let my farm stand. I know You can if you will."

John said that the Lord heard and answered that prayer, and the tornado made a U-turn around that farm. The farm with its crops, the children, and Aunt Sue were miraculously untouched. Aunt Sue's prayer had effected a miracle!

Miracles happen every day. Expect yours!

Lord, give us the conviction of all the Aunt Sues of the world. Help us to believe in the miraculous power of prayer. Amen.

The Miracle of Forwarding Mail

HAVE YOU EVER CONSIDERED how miraculous it is that mail delivered to the wrong address can be—and sometimes actually is—forwarded to the right address? Well, it is a miracle that Lurlene will not soon forget. Lurlene is a retired grandmother who uses her monthly retirement check to support her granddaughter. One month the check was late, and Lurlene called to inquire about it. She was informed that the check had been sent and was probably lost in the mail. All that could be done was to stop payment on the original check and issue another one. But this process would take some time, and she was advised to wait a few more days before ordering such action.

Lurlene was in a quandary, for she needed to buy food and pay her bills. She could not wait for a new check to be issued. Lurlene did the only thing she knew to do—she prayed. She knew that God knew her situation, and she did not believe that God would allow her and her granddaughter to remain in want.

Lurlene went to the mailbox hoping to find the much-needed check, but all she found was a letter from a woman named Hazel who lived in a place Lurlene had never heard of—Boston, Georgia. The letter was definitely addressed to her, with the correct spelling of her full name and the correct address. Carefully examining the letter, she found these words printed on the back: "It is better to give thanks and praise the Lord." When she opened it, she found her missing check. It seems that her check was attached to Hazel's, and both had been mailed to Hazel.

Hazel had assisted God in performing the miracle for which Lurlene had prayed. This piece of forwarded mail was indeed miraculous in Lurlene's sight. When she went to the bank to deposit the check, the bank clerk said, "You must be a good, praying woman, for God truly blessed you."

Lurlene replied, "I try to be."

Miracles happen every day. Expect yours!

Lord, teach us to be honest in forwarding that which does not belong to us. We may be helping to perform a miracle. Amen.

The Miracle of Fasting

DELLA'S MOTHER WAS DIAGNOSED as having breast cancer. This was indeed distressing news, but Della knew that it was simply a diagnosis. She remembered having read, "Truly I tell you, if you say to this mountain, 'Be taken up and thrown into the sea,' and if you do not doubt in your heart, but believe that what you say will come to pass, it will be done for you. So I tell you, whatever you ask for in prayer, believe that you have received it, and it will be yours" (Mark 11:23–24).

Believing in her heart that the cancer, like a mountain, could be taken up and thrown into the sea, Della decided to fast and pray for her mother. For fourteen days she ate nothing and drank only water. She kept reading the Scriptures and believing in her heart that her mother could and would be cured. She kept imagining being able to testify in church before other believers so that their faith might be strengthened. She knew there would be rejoicing over her faith victory.

Fully confident that the cancer had been removed, Della accompanied her mother to the doctor for an examination. Just as she expected, the lump was gone. There was no sign of cancer. Had the initial diagnosis been wrong or had the mountain been moved?

Della believes the Scriptures. She asked in prayer and fasting, believed that it would be hers, and it was. Praise God!

Miracles happen every day. Expect yours!

Lord, strengthen our faith so that we will be able to move mountains. Amen.

The Miracle of Repair

DON WOOD HEADS THE VIDEO and television operation for the United Methodist Church at Good News Television in Macon, Georgia. He is a communications specialist who has been in the television business for twenty years. During a recent taping at the station, he told me about the miracle of repair.

It seems that when Don first got started in the television business, he was working with an extremely temperamental camera. It often would not work properly and had to be taken to the shop for repairs. He just did not know how he would be able to complete his assignments with one camera constantly on the blink.

One day an elderly woman came to the studio, and that camera chose precisely that time to stop working. Don apologized for the inconvenience and told the woman that the camera often got sick. The woman simply said, "Well, I guess we will just have to pray for its cure." Don did not want to discourage the woman, so he remained quiet while she asked God to cure the camera of its ills and to keep it in good working condition.

Prior to that prayer, the camera had not worked more than one week without breaking down. After that prayer, the camera ran for one and one-half years without any problem.

Don admits that he had never thought of praying for a camera. He had always reserved his prayers for people. But that old woman's prayer worked, for miraculously the camera was repaired. It was a miracle of repair.

Miracles happen every day. Expect yours!

Lord, our prayers are always meaningful, even when they are for things. We know that everything that is comes under Your control. Amen.

The Miracle of Peace

JOYCE WAS SCARED. She had been in terrible pain, and the doctors had determined that she had a uterine mass that had doubled in size in ten days. Immediate surgery was necessary, but her being RH negative complicated things. There was no blood available for the surgery, and it could not be performed without it. Her church put out an alert, and the two pints necessary were donated.

Joyce's fear accelerated when she thought of her sister, who had died of a similar ailment. Her mother's tears affirmed the fear that another child would be lost to painful death.

Then a miracle of peace came over Joyce. She recounted her life. She had beautiful, successful children; she had a loving husband and lived in a lovely home; she had good friends and was completing her doctorate in psychology. She knew that if it was God's will that she die, she had lived fully.

Two days before her surgery, I talked to Joyce. She told me about the peace that had come over her. She asked for prayer, but she said that she was happier than she had ever been and she was ready if God was. I told her not to claim death but life. I knew that the death of her body would mean eternal life of her spirit, but I felt that her earthly life had not been completed.

On the day of her surgery, I periodically prayed that she would be spared and that the mass would not be cancerous. I asked other believers to join with me in prayer. I remembered that the prayers of the righteous avail much. I just hoped that our prayers would be within the will of God.

Joyce's surgery was successful. The mass was not cancerous. She will have an opportunity to continue her life on earth, but she had accepted her fate. She had found peace, and it was a miracle.

Miracles happen every day. Expect yours!

Lord, help us to be content, at peace, in whatever state we find ourselves. Amen.

The Miracle of Revival

ON JANUARY 3, 1994, George had a massive heart attack. He and his wife, Marla, had gone to the bank, but because he was not feeling well, they stopped by the fire station for oxygen. He collapsed at the station. He was in cardiac arrest and had no vital signs. From all indications, he was dead. But the firemen continued to work with him, and Marla prayed. She asked God to let him live a little longer. She kept telling God that she was not ready for him to go. Ten minutes passed, and then there was a miracle of revival. Joe's heart started to beat again.

George was admitted to the hospital where the medical personnel continued to work on him for three hours. Two days later, George was sitting up, eating, and talking to Marla. During his medical examinations, a bleeding ulcer was discovered, and with that added complication, George was labeled the "Miracle Man."

In February, just one month later, George had another heart attack. Although this attack was not as serious as the first one, his heart was so badly weakened that the cardiologist recommended a heart transplant.

George still waits for a donor heart. He is still the "Miracle Man," the one who experienced the miracle of revival.

Miracles happen every day. Expect yours!

Lord, thank You for a few more days to serve You. Revive us, awaken us, help us to make the most of our gift of life. Amen.

The Miracle of Coupons

TWO OF HELEN AND WALTER'S three daughters were in college at the same time. Money was extremely tight. There was hardly enough for groceries, but they had decided to sacrifice whatever they had to in order to secure an education for their daughters.

Seeing that there was little food in the house, Helen sat down to make up a grocery list. She tried to be as careful as possible. She only wrote down the bare necessities, but still her list was long. When she handed the list to her husband, he told her that there was no way that his money would meet her list. She told him that she had prayed, and that somehow God would provide. Walter also believed in prayer, but he wanted her to cut some of the items from the list. He did not want to be embarrassed at the grocery store, having to give back items because he could not pay for them. Helen told him that she could not cut the list; she needed everything on it.

Walter kept waiting for Helen to revise the list, and Helen kept praying. Then she thought about the coupons she had been saving. She started matching the coupons with the items on the list. To her amazement, there was a coupon for almost every item. Armed with the coupons, Walter went to the store, bought everything on the list, and had a little change left over. The fact that they had been able to purchase all of their groceries with a little money and a lot of coupons was a miracle.

Miracles happen every day. Expect yours!

Lord, teach us to have faith in Your ability to provide when we use what we have. Amen.

The Miracle of Salvation

ON JULY 4, 1976, Mary made a conscious decision to surrender her life to Christ. She was seeking salvation, and the only way she knew to do it was to write a letter to Jesus surrendering all that she had to him.

Mary started by listing all the clothes that she had, and she really did love clothes. Then she listed all of her real estate holdings and household possessions. She wrote in her letter to Jesus that she did not want anything except salvation. Mary surrendered her jewelry and her bank accounts; she even surrendered her husband and children. She literally wanted Jesus to take control of her entire life.

Feeling relieved, Mary entered into prayer, asking for salvation. A wonderful feeling of peace invaded her body. She felt redeemed. There was nothing her husband or children could say or do, for she knew that she had been saved. When they asked her what was wrong, she told them that she was at peace, for she had been redeemed by the blood of the Lamb.

Mary continued to write letters to her Lord. Whenever she was in need of counsel, she wrote it down. She found her writing to be a source of strength and deliverance. She knew that being saved would not exempt her from life's troubles, but she felt equipped to deal with them.

Her husband went to church with her and asked the minister to help him get the peace that his wife had. He wanted his life to change in the same way that his wife's had. But the minister explained that the peace his wife had came only from Jesus. No one else could give it to him, and no one could take it away. Mary's husband began to pray for salvation. As Mary joined him in prayer, he felt the very special love and peace that only comes with salvation.

Mary feels that the salvation that came to her household through surrender was a miracle. But that miracle was promised, for Jesus said, "When you [are converted], strengthen your brothers" (Luke 22:32). The miracle of salvation awaits us all if those who are converted will strengthen their brothers and sisters.

Miracles happen every day. Expect yours!

Lord, thank You for the salvation that is offered to all who surrender their lives to You. Amen.

The Miracle of Surrender

LIKE MARY, TERRI ALSO EXPERIENCED a miracle after she decided to surrender her life to Christ. She was a graduate student who had been working in a part-time capacity for Northern Telecom, and she had very little money. In spite of her circumstances, she decided to tithe, fast one day a week, and pray. The decision to tithe was a big one. Sometimes the money she used to pay her tithe was money she needed for bills, but she knew that all of the money belonged to God and He deserved His first. Having surrendered all that she had and all that she was to Christ, she had learned to trust Him for her needs.

Continuing to be faithful to her decisions to tithe, fast, and pray, Terri discovered that she was being asked to work more hours and her family was helping her more. She was never late with a payment on her bills, and she felt the spirit of peace that only comes from surrender.

After completing her graduate degree, Terri was offered a full-time job working five days a week at thirty dollars an hour. Of course, she was thrilled, but she knew that it would take her years to pay off her thirty thousand dollar debt in loans. When she explained her debt to her supervisor, Terri was permitted to work extra hours to help with her indebtedness. Eventually, all loans were repaid.

Terri is convinced that her act of surrender resulted in the miracles that have constantly been a part of her life. She has had other jobs, and with each job she has felt that God has been in control. She has even had the luxury of turning down jobs that she did not feel were right for her, and each time God has shown her a better way. She has remained faithful in her commitment to fast, tithe, and pray. It is a miracle, a miracle of surrender.

Miracles happen every day. Expect yours!

Lord, lead us all toward surrender. All that we have and all that we are belongs to You. Take it and use it and us to Your glory. Amen.

The Miracle of Independence

MARTHA IS A DRUG ADDICT. She needs a miracle of independence from her addiction. Her daughter, Danita, is praying for that miracle, and Martha is recovering.

Martha's addiction began in 1983 with marijuana. Then she tried harder drugs. Danita was only nine years old, but she knew that her mother was sick. She pleaded with Martha to stop using drugs. Danita was committed to doing whatever she could to make her mother well; she even began to pray. Then one day Martha stopped taking drugs. Danita was so happy, for she knew that God had answered her prayers.

During the following five-year reprieve, Danita's little brother and sister were born. Danita is not sure how or why it happened, but her mother started using drugs again. Martha neglected the care of her children. She would spend the day-care and food money on drugs; she would leave the children with anyone while she searched the streets for a hit. Whenever things did not work out to her liking and satisfaction, Martha would blame Danita. As a young teenager, Danita did not know how to cope with an addicted mother and two small siblings. All Danita could do was pray. Danita prayed that this time her mother could get off drugs and stay off. She prayed for a miracle of independence from drugs.

Danita knew that as long as she lived with her mother, her mother would depend on her to care for the younger children. Danita felt that if she left, her mother might realize the danger she was putting her children in while she was high. Danita left home, but she kept praying for her mother. Slowly Martha started to recover. She started attending church regularly, reading her Bible, and attending Bible study classes.

Danita is still praying for her mother. She says that she refuses to allow that cocaine devil to destroy her mother. Danita has claimed her miracle, the miracle of her mother's independence from drugs.

Miracles happen every day. Expect yours!

Lord, thank You for children who pray for their parents. We realize the truth in "a little child shall lead them." Amen.

The Miracle of Intercession

KAREN HAD MONONUCLEOSIS. She was very sick, having a constant fever and sore throat and feeling completely exhausted. She had been to a doctor, who had treated her and expected her to recover in a couple of weeks. But Karen got worse. Her throat glands were so swollen that she could not swallow, and her ear had become infected. Her doctor recommended a throat specialist, for he had never seen a case that had become so severe. He felt certain that the specialist would have to cut the infection out.

Karen's mother, Helen, was worried. Her daughter could not eat or drink and had already lost eleven pounds from her thin ninety-three-pound frame. Helen had been praying for Karen, but her prayers did not seem to be enough. She thought about asking others to pray also. She had heard of a little Pentecostal church where there were intercessory prayer and healing services every Wednesday night. She decided to go.

At that Pentecostal church, Helen had a religious experience she would never forget. The worshipers were singing and praying and speaking in tongues. She felt the presence of the Holy Spirit, and after the sermon, worshipers were invited to come to the altar for healing. Helen went to the altar as a proxy for Karen to ask for healing. The minister and some of the worshipers anointed Helen as they laid hands on her and prayed for Karen's healing. While the worshipers praised God, Helen silently prayed, "God, forgive me. I didn't mean to use these beautiful people. But Karen needs help. She is so sick. And You said, 'Where two or three are gathered in My name—ask and it will be given you.' We are asking. Please, God, heal her—if it is Your will. If she is not healed, I will know You have some other purpose, and we will accept it. I ask in Jesus' name." This intercessory prayer and healing service took place at 9:00 P.M.

When Helen returned home, she found Karen sitting at the kitchen table, doing what she had not been able to do for days—eating. She had a big smile on her face. The miracle of healing that had taken place was simply unbelievable. God had revealed to Karen that Helen had asked the people to pray for her and that Helen had acted as proxy for her by receiving the anointing and feeling the laying on of hands. Karen also knew that this service had taken place at 9:00 P.M., because at that time she had vomited the bloody substance that was infecting her throat and keeping her from eating and drinking.

Karen kept her appointment with the doctor, and he confirmed her healing and admitted that a miracle had taken place. It was a miracle of intercessory prayer.

Miracles happen every day. Expect yours!

Lord, You have told us to join together in prayer. When we agree in spirit and are united in Your name, miracles happen. Amen.

The Miracle of Certification

GAIL HAD ALWAYS WANTED to be a kindergarten teacher. She had just started the last year of her graduate program, and she knew that she could complete her degree and pass her certification in time for the opening of the next school year. She was especially excited because her father would be so proud of her. He had always encouraged her and told her that she would be a fine teacher. She looked forward to being able to show him her certificate.

But Gail's world began to fall apart when her father was diagnosed with terminal cancer. She could not concentrate on her studies. She wanted to spend as much time as possible with her dying father. She dropped out of school for a short period just before her father died, but she still tried to finish her degree. Although she finished her program in August, she did not have time to take and pass the certification process.

Gail refused to give up her dream. She heard about the possibility of teaching on a provisional certificate for one year. She was interviewed and got a job as a kindergarten teacher. She knew that her job was only provisional, and she proceeded to make plans to take the certification test so that her position would be secure. Although she took the test, she did not receive the results. Her first year ended, and she was not offered a position for the next year because she was not certified and there was no record of her having taken the test. The principal for whom she had worked wanted to offer her a contract, but he could not. He sent her to the Board of Education, hoping that they could find out what had happened to her test. There was no word on either the test or her score.

The Friday before the teachers were to report for the new school year, Gail had still not heard about her certification. She knew that she would not be offered a contract without some proof of her having taken and passed the test. She also knew that her principal would have to fill the position with someone else. She hoped and prayed that her test results would be in that day's mail. It was her last chance.

Gail and her mother met in the family kitchen at 1:00 P.M. Their mail usually was delivered about 3:00 P.M. They prayed that it would miraculously come early so Gail would have time to take the results to the Board of Education. She and her mother had already claimed her having passed. They got down on their knees and prayed that the letter they needed would arrive. While they were on their knees, the mail came and Gail's letter contained the information she needed. She had passed with flying colors.

Gail was able to reach both the Board of Education and her principal in time to be certified and hired for the new school year. She says that for the first time in her life she knew how real God was in her life, and she feels compelled to witness to others. For her the events were miraculous!

Miracles happen every day. Expect yours!

Lord, help us to believe in prayer and in Your presence at work in our lives. Amen.

The Miracle of the Dent

JANICE AND HER COLLEGE ROOMMATES rented a car in which to take a weekend trip. None of the girls had very much money, and they had borrowed a charge card to rent the car, so they were very careful and very prayerful as they drove the car off the lot. They prayed that they would have a safe journey and that they would not injure or be injured by anyone. They also prayed that they would return the car without damage.

The girls had a safe trip, and they were on their way to return the car when they had an accident. Janice was driving, and she briefly took her eyes off the road. The car in front of her stopped suddenly, and Janice hit it. The girls were devastated. How would they pay for damage? How could this have happened? How would they tell their parents?

They all got out of the car to inspect the damage. The woman driving the car they had hit was very understanding. She did not notice any damage to her car and told them to forget it. But there was a big dent in the rental car. What would they do?

They went home, called the rental company, and were told to call the police to report the accident. But the police told them that since they had left the scene of the accident, there was not much point in their submitting a report. They were advised to call their insurance company. That is when they got nervous. What insurance company? This was a rental car. They decided to take the car back to the rental agency and let them inspect the damage. They prayed that they would be able to pay for it and they thanked God that the damage was not any worse and that no one had been hurt.

When they went outside to return the car, the dent was gone. There was only a scratch in its place. What had happened to the dent? Was this some kind of miraculous answer to their prayers? When the attendant checked their car in, he said, "I thought you had had an accident. This scratch is nothing."

Janice says it was a miracle, for that big dent was really there. All of them saw it.

Well, Janice, miracles happen every day. Expect yours!

Lord, thank You for blessing us even in times when we are careless and accident prone. Your supply of miracles is always abundant. Amen.

The Miracle of Sixty-five Feet

DANNY WAS GUIDING HIS CHURCH GROUP on an outing at Tallulah Gorge State Park. In the last eighteen months, six people had died in falls and drownings at Tallulah Gorge, so Danny was warning everyone to be careful. Just as he was telling them that the rocks were wet and slippery, he slipped. He was on the ledge of a waterfall, sixty-five feet above big rocks and a pool called Devil's Foot Bath.

As he tumbled down the face of the waterfall, Danny knew he was going to die. All he saw were the big rocks. He could not even see the pool. He just closed his eyes and prayed. He prayed to survive the fall against all odds. He prayed for a sixty-five foot miracle.

He reached out to grab a ledge, hoping to help break his fall, and he landed in the pool. He was pulled unconscious from the water by a member of his church group and was taken to a nearby medical center. He had a deep head gash and a compressed fracture of a vertebra, but he had survived.

Danny's prayer had been answered. His miracle was one of sixty-five feet. Miracles happen every day. Expect yours!

Lord, You are able to effect miracles of unlimited types. Give us the faith to believe regardless of our circumstances. Amen.

The Miracle of Prayers with Legs

FOR THE PAST FEW YEARS, Ruth and Don had struggled to pay college tuition and associated expenses for their two daughters. But their resources had run dry, and they were not sure how they would be able to provide what was needed for the upcoming academic year. They prayed every day. They even prayed to win the lottery, but somehow they knew that God would use His own resources to answer their prayers.

Then they heard someone say, "Put legs on prayers." They took that to mean that you must do more than pray and sit around. After you pray, you must get up and hustle. So, Don started working harder in his small business and even got a part-time summer job. Ruth encouraged their daughters to apply for scholarships and to keep their grades up so that they would qualify. Both Ruth and Don felt that they were putting legs on their prayers.

Their small business started showing greater profits; the income from the part-time job could be directly applied to the college expenses, and one of their daughters was awarded not one but three scholarships for the coming academic year. God had answered their prayers. In fact, God had shown them the miracle of prayers with legs.

Miracles happen every day. Expect yours!

Lord, teach us to put legs on our prayers. You have given us legs to help us answer our own requests. We don't need to leave everything up to You. Amen.

The Miracle of a Home

JACKIE LIVED WITH HER MOTHER and siblings in an apartment that was too small and badly in need of repair. Her father had long since disappeared, and her mother was very ill. Jackie wondered how they would ever be able to move or even afford the repairs.

Jackie's mother told her children that they were not even going to try to fix up that old apartment; they were going to buy a house of their very own. Jackie wanted to believe her mother, but how could she? Her mother was receiving a very small income, and with the medical expenses, there was just not enough money to think about buying a house. But her mother was insistent.

Jackie started believing her mother. She noticed her mother praying for a house that she could make into a home for her children. She watched her mother seek resources wherever they could be found, and she could not resist joining her in prayer. But Jackie was not sure how prayer worked. Could prayer bring about the miracle of a home?

Jackie's mother told her children that through prayer all things are possible. She explained that God was already answering their prayers, for her health was improving, and soon she would be able to work an additional job. She told them to keep praying, and she would keep looking for a suitable house that they could claim as their home. Being obedient children, they did as they were told.

Jackie's mother found the perfect house. Now it was up to God to help them with their miracle. Church members and friends chipped in and, miraculously, they qualified for a loan and bought their house.

That house became a home as soon as they entered and fell down to praise and thank God. Jackie says that when anyone asks her how they got that home she replies, "On bended knee in prayer, how else?" It was indeed a miracle.

Miracles happen every day. Expect yours!

Lord, thank You for blessing those who believe that all things are possible through prayer. Amen.

The Miracle of the List

LYNN AND HER HUSBAND had lost their business and all of their money. They had not yet found jobs, and they had no food in the house. Lynn had always found comfort in prayer, and she kept remembering the verse, "I have been young, and now am old, yet I have not seen the righteous forsaken or their children begging bread" (Psalm 37:25). She thought to herself, *Lord, I have been faithful, and You promised that I would not have to beg for bread.*

Acting on her prayer, Lynn made out a list of groceries that she needed. She had no money, and she did not know how she would purchase the items on her list, but she stuck it on the refrigerator door and said, "These are our needs, Lord." Having done this, she left to look for work.

Lynn returned home to a house without food, but she noticed that the list was still on the refrigerator and that she still needed everything on that list. She sat at the kitchen table, wondering what she and her husband could possibly eat. The doorbell rang, and Lynn found some members of her church at the door with a box of groceries. They told her that the groceries had been left by someone for a needy family. They hoped that she would accept the food, for they knew she and her husband had some needs. Lynn was overjoyed, and she thanked them.

While she was putting the groceries away, she noticed that every item she had written down that morning on her wish list was there. It was a miracle! God had kept his promise.

Miracles happen every day. Expect yours!

Lord, help us to remember Your promises and to act in faith as You continuously supply our needs. Amen.

The Miracle of Blinking

DIANE HAS ALWAYS LIVED AN ACTIVE LIFE. She has delighted in spreading joy and has rejoiced in her ability as a good communicator. So when she noticed that she was losing control of her muscles and her ability to speak, she was quite distressed. She wondered how she would be able to communicate as her condition worsened, for she had been diagnosed with Lou Gehrig's disease.

Diane's husband, an engineer with an outstanding knowledge of computers, prayed for a solution as Diane lost her ability to speak to him. God led him to develop a special computer program that responded to the blinking of Diane's eyes. Diane would blink as the computer cursor landed on the letter she wanted to use to form the words she wanted to say. There were within the program some preset simple words and phrases that she could blink the cursor to without having to spell out the entire word. Diane also found out that the program her husband developed would respond to the rolling of her eyes from one side to the other. That was a signal to end a sentence. There were other eye movements that ended paragraphs and entire documents.

Communicating this way was time consuming, but it worked. Diane was still able to live her life of rejoicing as she made contact with her husband and family. All she had to do was blink. It was a miracle.

Miracles happen every day. Expect yours!

Lord, thank You for computer technology and for all the ways it helps us to communicate with one another. Amen.

The Miracle of Second Birth

IN 1991 SHERRY'S MOTHER experienced kidney failure. The continuation of her very life was dependent upon dialysis and a transplant operation. Neither option looked good. She had always been so active, and dialysis meant dependence on a machine. She did not want to be a slave to a machine. She could only imagine how limited her life and activities would be, and her chances of obtaining a compatible kidney transplant were one in ten. At least for the time being, she had to go with dialysis.

During the course of dialysis, she became very depressed. During visits, Sherry could see that her mother was experiencing a slow death. Bouts with pain accompanied by lingering doubts and greatly reduced activity worked to stifle her spirit. Sherry began to pray for a miracle.

On one of her limited trips to the store, Sherry's mother was approached by a woman whom she did not know. The woman said, "It's okay. Keep praying. Your prayers will be answered." The very next day Sherry's grandmother qualified as a kidney donor. Sherry knew that her grandmother represented the miracle for which she had prayed. Her grandmother would give her mother life twice, once by birth and again by donating a kidney.

It was in fact a miracle of second birth, for both mother and grandmother are well four years after a successful transplant. Sherry's mother is back to normal activities, and Sherry is thanking God for her miracle.

Miracles happen every day. Expect yours!

Lord, help us to listen for Your word and witness. Strangers sometimes bring us Your messages. May we not be faithless but believing. Amen.

Miraculous Blessings

The Miracle of the Gift

SEOLA MCCARTY is eighty-seven years old. She quit school in the sixth grade to go to work, and she never returned. She has been working on the same job, taking in dirty laundry and returning it clean and ironed, for many years. The miraculous thing is that she has spent almost none of the money she has made. She has never married or had children, eats little, buys few clothes, and neither owns nor knows how to drive a car. She also has conserved electricity, and she needs little besides her Bible to read and relax.

So, what has she done with the money she has managed to save? On her own she has decided to give it to her hometown University of Southern Mississippi to be used for scholarships for black students from southern Mississippi. Her gift, virtually all of her salary, amounted to one hundred and fifty thousand dollars, and it was matched by local business leaders. The resulting three hundred thousand dollars will provide scholarships into the indefinite future.

The executive director who administers donations for the University of Southern Mississippi Foundation says that this gift is truly a miracle. In his twenty-four years of working with private fund-raising, he has never experienced a gift like this from a person who was not affluent. Oseola gave the gift because, when she was young, her race could not go to that college; now, since its integration three decades ago, they can.

Oseola asks only that she be allowed to attend the graduation of some young person who has made it through college because of her gift. She says that she would like to see it.

The first student to be awarded her scholarship has met Oseola and has adopted her as a grandmother. Although that student's family made too much money to qualify for a federal grant, they did not make enough to afford her college tuition. For them, the gift was a miracle.

Miracles happen every day. Expect yours!

Lord, thank You for those unselfish persons who are willing to make miracles happen for others. Amen.

The Miracle of Wedding Finances

TERRI HAD PRAYED FOR A HUSBAND. She had asked God to reveal him to her, for she knew that God had someone special for her. She had been told by a minister whom she accidentally met at the train station that she would be engaged in three days and married within the year. Terri was dating someone, but she was not sure that he was the one God had chosen for her. When he asked her to marry him three days after she had met the minister, she felt that God had spoken. It was time to plan the wedding.

Having just completed graduate school, Terri had no money. How could she have a wedding with no money? Again she asked God to direct her. She surrendered herself and all of her needs to God. She knew that God had all of the money and all of the resources that she needed to have the type of wedding she desired. She was led to ask her parents how much they could contribute, and they told her that all they could afford was five hundred dollars. Terri decided that if God wanted her to have a five hundred dollar wedding, then that was what she would do.

But Terri's grandmother heard of her wedding plans and called to tell her that she had two thousand five hundred dollars to contribute. She asked only that Terri use a little of that money to buy her grandmother's dress and shoes for the wedding. Terri gladly agreed. Then both her great-aunt and another aunt called, each offering a one thousand dollar contribution. Finally, the groom's mother called to offer two thousand dollars for the honeymoon and whatever was needed for the rehearsal dinner. Terri knew that miraculously God had provided the wedding finances. Thanks be to God.

Miracles happen every day. Expect yours!

Lord, if we but surrender ourselves to You, You will supply our needs. Amen.

The Miracle of Timing

PART OF THE TIME THAT I WORKED in corporate America, I worked for a privately held computer software company. The company became very successful, and a decision was made to become a public company. Many employees held stock in the company, and once it went public, we had to pay taxes on our stock. The company agreed to lend us the money for the taxes, but we had to make a commitment not to sell our stock for two years and to remain as employees or forfeit the stock. After that two-year period, we could sell enough of the stock to repay our loans. Most of us agreed to the terms.

The company continued to prosper, and after the two years, we all repaid our loans. Then we were in a position to hold our stock or sell as much as we wanted. At that point I made a prayerful decision. I calculated the balance on our family home mortgage, and I calculated the amount I would need my stock to sell for in order to liquidate that balance. I needed each share to sell for eighteen dollars.

The price of the stock rose rapidly, and I kept waiting for the right moment to sell. I prayed that God would bless the company and give me the opportunity to free our family from the burden of a monthly mortgage payment.

Many employees calculated the amount of money they had on paper, and they dreamed of getting rich. I only wanted to get out of debt. They laughed at me, and told me that if I sold at eighteen dollars a share, I would miss having all the money they would have, for they expected the stock to continue to rise.

But I understand greed, and I know that when you wait too long, you can miss your blessings. Somehow it seems that there is a window of opportunity, and you can miss it by trying to wait for a better time.

Just before I left on a business trip, the stock had got very close to eighteen dollars a share. While I was away, the stock had passed eighteen dollars and had risen to nineteen dollars. I immediately sent my stock certificates to my broker with the instructions to sell all of my shares. By the time my broker received them, the stock had risen to twenty-two dollars and fifty cents per share. My broker called and asked if I was sure that I wanted to sell, because the stock was still going up. I told him that I was sure. We sold at twenty-two dollars and fifty cents per share, which was the highest the stock ever rose. By the next week, the stock had dropped to five dollars per share.

Everyone wanted to know how I knew when to sell. I told them that I had set a goal, had asked God to bless me, and had promised to carry through without greed. It was very simply a miracle, a miracle of timing.

Miracles happen every day. Expect yours!

Lord, keep us from greed and obsession with material riches. We are abundantly rich when we put our faith and trust in You. Amen.

The Miracle of New Shoes

AFTER PLAYING THE PIANO for a worship service, Lynne was handed some money by one of the parishioners, who told her to go buy some new shoes. Not only was she amazed by the admonition, she was somewhat embarrassed. It was true; her shoes were in terrible condition, but she had no idea that anyone would notice them.

Lynne started not to take the money. Then she remembered the Bible verse, "If God so clothes the grass of the field, which is alive today and tomorrow is thrown into the oven, will he not much more clothe you—you of little faith?" (Matthew 6:30). Just two days earlier she had given most of her money to support the church's building program, and as she was giving the money she had said, "God, it's Your money, not mine. I know You will provide what I need." Now Lynne wondered whether she had really meant that when she said it, for God was, through this parishioner, providing what she needed. This was her miracle, her blessing, the answer to her prayer. So she expressed her thanks, put the money in her pocket, and headed to the store to buy her much needed new shoes.

Miracles happen every day. Expect yours!

Lord, help me to recognize and accept my miracles when they happen. You do provide all we need. Amen.

The Miracle of Graduation

ON MAY 30, 1994, MONA FREYE, a seventy-eight-year-old grandmother, graduated from the University of California at Berkeley. It was a miracle! How had this seventy-eight-year-old woman managed to survive the arthritis that often had made it difficult to walk to class? How had she managed to tape record all of the lectures that her aching fingers had made too painful to write? How had she forced herself to reread the many chapters that her frequent memory losses had wiped away? It was a miracle!

Mona was determined. She wanted the college degree that poverty and racial discrimination had deprived her. She wanted to be a role model for her grandchildren. She wanted to succeed, and her very spirit of determination had been the motivation to the fulfillment of her miracle.

Mona knew that the road would not be easy. She had to work her way through college, and fortunately she found a job in the university's college reentry program. What a wonderful example she was of college reentry! I am sure that just seeing her and knowing that a woman of her age was in college encouraged others to reenter.

In her United States history class, Mona was able to contribute to class discussions by giving practical examples of her own survival of the Depression. Most of her classmates had not been born during the years about which they studied. But Mona remembered those lean years and could make the pages of the text live.

Is there a graduation that you would like to experience? Do you think you are too old, too feeble, too dumb to make it happen? Or are you expecting your miracle? Mona was, and hers became a reality.

Miracles happen every day. Expect yours!

Lord, with Your help, all things are possible—even graduation at seventy-eight. Thank You. Amen.

The Miracle of Opportunity

DELVECCHIO IS A TEENAGER growing up in one of Atlanta's public housing projects. He is surrounded by poverty, drugs, and the crimes associated with his environment. But Delvecchio has an opportunity to rise above his circumstances. He has God-given talents, and he has met some friends who have exposed him to a better way of life.

Delvecchio's miracle of opportunity began at birth. God blessed him with a rich and melodious voice that earned him a place in the fine arts department of his high school. God also gave him brains that he has used to qualify as a student in the Academy of Math and Science of that high school. He has a straight A average and has scored over twelve hundred on the SAT college entrance examination. His God-given leadership skills have allowed him to distinguish himself as a student leader and community volunteer. He volunteers with the county hospital's Teen Services Program, counseling eighth-graders about delaying early sexual involvement.

All of his gifts have provided Delvecchio with the opportunity to attend college on a full scholarship. Just being exposed to other teens from middle-class families at his high school academy has opened new horizons for Delvecchio. He knows that it is possible to live a safer, more fruitful life outside the boundaries of his housing project. College will further broaden his horizons.

Delvecchio plans to attend medical school after college and wants to provide the miracle of opportunity for his younger brother. He knows what a low income life is, and he is thankful for the opportunity his talents have provided. It is indeed a miracle!

Miracles happen every day. Expect yours!

Lord, help us to encourage Young people who seek to rise above their circumstances, and make us ever mindful of those who have helped and encouraged us. Amen.

The Miracle of Water

CASCADE UNITED METHODIST CHURCH had outgrown its building. The members were committed to building a new place of worship. They had purchased land and had secured a contractor, but they were not hooked up to the city water system. It would take some time before the city water would be available, and time was precious. The old building had been sold, and the members were renting another building until their new one was available. They were ready to build, but they could not build without water.

Surveying the land, they discovered a spring that ran crystal clear just east of the building site. The contractors dug a hole, inserted a fifty-five gallon drum, and continuously pumped all of the water they needed—free of charge. The water they pumped was so pure that some of the workers drank daily from the spring. The new church building was eighty percent completed before the site was connected to the city water system.

It was only after the building was completed that the spring water ceased to run clear. As the Cascade members reflect upon the miracle water, they realize that God provided the water for the building of His church; and, after it was completed, the miracle water was no longer needed. Cascade continues to thank God for providing that miracle water.

Miracles happen every day. Expect yours!

Lord, there has always been something miraculous and life-saving about water. Thank You for providing it for us so that we may live to serve and worship You. Amen.

The Miracle of Monetary Assistance

ISAIAH'S GRANDFATHER DIED SUDDENLY and unexpectedly. The family had to make rapid arrangements to travel from Georgia to Florida for the funeral. Being a closely knit family, they pooled their resources so that all of the family members could attend the funeral.

Once they arrived in Florida, they discovered that there was not sufficient insurance to cover the cost of the funeral. They all made donations. They also had to raise the money needed for food and lodging during their Florida stay. Each family member had to contribute a share of the total cost. When they returned to Georgia, they could clearly feel their financial distress.

But before they could resume their normal lives and replenish their financial coffers, their young cousin died of a massive heart attack. Funeral arrangements started again. And again, there was no money for the funeral. No one had expected their cousin to die at such an early age, and of course, no one expected him to die so soon after their grandfather's death. There was just no money. The whole family was broke.

Just when the family was at its most desperate point, the employees of the hotel where their cousin had worked took up a collection and presented Isaiah's family with more than enough money to cover the funeral expenses. They all believe it was a miracle!

Miracles happen every day. Expect yours!

Lord, thank You for Christians who lend a helping hand in times of need. Amen.

The Miracle Fall

IN 1990, AS MRS. WILSON and her children were leaving their house, she fell. Her fall was sudden and unexpected. She did not slip or trip; she just blacked out. When she regained consciousness, her children insisted on taking her to the hospital. Although she protested that she was only unconscious for a few seconds and that she was fine, her children prevailed.

Because she had fallen on her hip, an X ray was taken. The doctors said that there might be some soreness, but there were no fractures. Acting on impulse or miraculous insight, the doctor asked permission to do a CAT scan. The scan revealed a tumor on the pituitary gland, and emergency surgery was required. The tumor was removed before it had an opportunity to permanently harm or kill Mrs. Wilson.

Her children are thankful that their mother fell because that fall put them in touch with an insightful doctor who was able to diagnose the real problem. It was a miraculous fall!

Miracles happen every day. Expect yours!

Lord, thank You for medical personnel who are concerned about their patients and who are willing to trust the insights You give them as they seek to assist in healing. Amen.

The Miracle of Walking

IRINA SHALIGINA HAD BEEN TRYING to get to her grandmother's house. Although she had taken the train part of the way, she needed to travel by bus the remaining five or six miles. The bus she needed was not running, so she decided to walk and got lost taking a shortcut through the woods. She walked and crawled through snowdrifts that were chest high. Snow collected in her high boots, and she had to survive by drinking melted snow. Having to spend two days and two nights exposed to the twenty degrees below zero temperatures common in the area of Russia in which she lived, she developed frostbite. Her legs were amputated about four inches below her knees as a treatment for the severe frostbite. Irina, fifteen years old, felt utter despair. She could not walk.

While she was in the hospital, Irina met Truett Dodd, a missionary with Campus Crusade for Christ. Truett said, "She never would have had a future. My heart just went out to her." Truett contacted a prosthetics and orthotics company based in Alpharetta, Georgia, and an offer was made to outfit Irina with artificial limbs free of charge.

Arrangements were made for Irina to be flown to the United States. The first night in her temporary home she crawled on the floor. The next day she moved about in a wheelchair. And three days later, with her stumps in the sockets of two artificial limbs, she began walking on parallel bars.

Irina says that she did not realize walking was a miracle until she had to crawl.

Miracles happen every day. Expect yours!

Lord, thank You for those who respond to disparity. Help us to realize that we assist You in effecting miracles as we find needs and fill them. Amen.

The Miracle of Help

LILLY AND AIDA ARE SISTERS who live together. They also are senior citizens. At the beginning of 1994, both women were in fairly good health, even though Aida had only one leg. She had lost a leg to diabetes several years before, but she could get around some with the help of crutches. But on April 25, 1994, Aida's second leg was amputated, and she was completely immobile. Lilly found it increasingly difficult to care for her sister.

Then, as so often happens with caregivers, Lilly's health failed. She was hospitalized, and there was no one to care for Aida. Lilly worried so much about her sister that her own recovery was hampered. Several family members took turns taking care of Aida, but there was no permanent solution.

Help came in the form of a group called Quality Living for Senior

Citizens. It was a miracle, a miracle of help. When Lilly was released from the hospital, she found that this group came to her home to offer help five days a week. The group provided food, cleaning, shopping, and transportation for both women to receive medical care. Lilly never thought it was possible to receive such help. She tells everyone about the miracle of help, and about how grateful she is to God.

Miracles happen every day. Expect yours!

Lord, thank You for groups like Quality Living that provide for the senior citizens among us. May we be more appreciative of the help they provide. Amen.

The Miracle of Disability

FOR FIFTY YEARS LUELLA LIVED in a healthy body, but she was not at peace. She was constantly searching for that unknown something that would make life full and happy. How could she find what she was looking for? Her eyes were normal, but she could not see. Her mind was good, but she could not discover the answers she sought. She was alive, but she was not living. She was only going through the motions. She was lost and did not know how to be found.

Then she suffered a disabling spinal injury. She was confined to her bed, and she had time to read the Bible, pray, and commune with God. Even as she endured severe pain, she felt a peace she had never known before. She had come to the realization of the love of God. How had she not seen it before? How could she have been so blind?

Friends came to visit Luella, and they noted the change in her personality.

She was kinder, more loving, more forgiving, and more like Christ. Being around her was pure joy. They were compelled to respond in like manner, demonstrating to Luella the power of God's love. She had learned that love begets love. She realized that you reap what you sow. How could she have not known that before? She had always thought of sowing and reaping in the negative sense, but she had discovered that it works in the positive sense also.

Today Luella walks with a cane. She has been disabled for seventeen years. Although she is still in pain, she realizes that God has miraculously blessed her. Her last seventeen years have made up for the first fifty that she spent as a lost soul.

Do we really have to become disabled in order to realize the miracle of living within the love of God?

Miracles happen every day. Expect yours!

Lord, teach us to love You, praise You, and serve You in every way, in sickness and in health. Amen.

The Miracle of Organ Donation

WHILE NICHOLAS GREEN WAS SLEEPING in the back of his parents' car as his family traveled toward Sicily on vacation, he was struck in the head by a bullet fired by highway bandits. Nicholas fell into a coma, and within three days was pronounced brain-dead. His grieving parents decided to use his death to effect a miracle for five young Italians. They donated Nicholas' liver, kidneys, heart, corneas, and pancreas for transplant operations.

The Italian people, who were devastated that someone vacationing in their country could be brutally and senselessly murdered, could not believe in the generosity of the family. The rate of organ donation is lower in Italy than it is in other developed countries, so the donations were especially welcome. Italian officials gave the Greens two medals and returned them to their Bodega Bay, California, home on a military plane.

When interviewed, the family stated that the vacation had followed a summer of studying ancient history, and that Julius Caesar had been Nicholas' hero. They felt certain that Nicholas would have wanted to help others, and his mother said, "I hope his heart lives a long time."

Although his death was a tragedy, it was the source of a miraculous gift for five young persons who needed a miracle of organ donation. Perhaps the example set by Nicholas' family will inspire others to effect similar miracles for others.

Miracles happen every day. Expect yours!

Lord, lead us to use even the most tragic situations to witness to the glory and power of Your love. Amen.

The Miracle Shooting

JIM WAS CAUGHT UP IN ILLEGAL ACTIVITIES. He sold drugs and was interested in making money any way possible. He was surrounded by all the things his money could buy. But he was not satisfied; he wanted more. He decided he could have more by cheating his drug suppliers. He was shot four times when his suppliers discovered his deception.

One of the bullets was imbedded in his head. Surgery was necessary, but he survived. After a lengthy hospital stay, during which he had an opportunity to think about his life, Jim walked out of the hospital with no long-term physical effects. But the mental, spiritual, and emotional effects were long lasting. Jim was convinced that God had used that shooting to help him change his life. He joined a church, found an honest but low-paying job, and constantly prayed that God would keep him on the straight and narrow path.

Today Jim is working with young people, telling his story, winning others for Christ, and talking about the miracle that occurred in his life because he was shot. That shooting changed his life. He is convinced that God can use anything to get your attention, and the shooting got his. It was a miracle!

Miracles happen every day. Expect yours!

Lord, help us to reach out to Young people who feel that life consists of material possessions. Make us effective witnesses to the happiness and fulfillment that is ours through spiritual alignment with You. Amen.

Miraculous Encounters

The Miracle of Witness

HE LIVED ON THE MEXICAN ISLAND of Isla Muheres, and she was only ten years old. She helped to support her family by selling gum and handmade items to tourists. She approached our group of four during our vacation visit. Having had four years of Spanish in high school, I started a conversation with her. My Spanish was very rusty, and her English was limited, but we managed to have a discussion of the jewelry that the various members of our group were wearing.

I noticed that the child was wearing a cross, and she noticed that three of the four in our group were also wearing crosses. She asked me why the fourth person was not wearing a cross. Interestingly enough, that person was my husband, who was the only ordained clergyperson among us.

My husband got the message. When we are among those with whom we are not conversing, the wearing of the cross is a witness. It identifies its wearers as members of the body of Christ, Christians. The little girl felt comfortable among fellow Christians, and she wanted the entire group to belong to the family of God with which she was identified.

After that encounter, my husband wore his cross, and he even questioned the practice among some clergy of keeping their crosses in their shirt pockets when not performing liturgical acts. The Christian witness needs to be constant. Christians need to be identified. Someone may need that miracle of witness.

Miracles happen every day. Expect yours!

Lord, help me to consciously witness to my faith every day, everywhere I am. May my witness not only be seen in the symbols I wear, but also in the life I live. Amen.

The Miracle of the Back Page

RUTH HAD JUST REMARRIED. Together she and her new husband had five daughters. Two of the girls were Ruth's daughters from a former marriage, and three were her husband's daughters. This blended family had difficulty adjusting. Ruth's daughters were resentful of their new stepfather and the attention that their mother was lavishing on him and his daughters. Ruth's stepdaughters were resentful of her for taking their dead mother's place, not only in their lives but also in their father's life. Ruth felt caught in the middle, pleasing no one.

And there were more than emotional adjustments; there also were financial adjustments. United, they suddenly had become a large family with hardly enough money to survive. Ruth was operating on a very strict budget, so she was very happy when she noticed that the back page of the newspaper was filled with coupons. She knew that those coupons would help her make the purchases her family needed within the budget.

Just before Ruth left for the store, the girls got into a big argument. They were yelling at one another and at Ruth. Ruth was very upset and left the house in tears, forgetting the back page with the needed coupons. When she realized her plight, she was outside the supermarket. She decided that she could not bear returning to the house where the shouting continued. She needed some time of solitude and peace, but how could she get everything she needed without that back page?

Ruth prayed that God would somehow find a way for her to make the necessary purchases and also have the much-needed time away from her family. She entered the store, believing that God would provide. No sooner than she was inside the store, a man touched her arm and said, "Here, I believe you need this." The man handed her the back page. There were all the coupons she needed.

Ruth turned to thank the man, but he had disappeared. Ruth believes he was an angel God sent to deliver her coupons. It was a miracle. The God she believes in cared enough to send coupons. He does supply every need.

Miracles happen every day. Expect yours!

Lord, thank You for loving us enough to send what we need. Amen.

The Miracle of Hesitation

IT HAS BEEN SAID THAT ANGELS are messengers of God, created on behalf of humans. Lynn believes that. She believes that God sent an angel to give her a message of hesitation.

As Lynn approached the intersection, the traffic light turned red and she stopped. She would be the first one to go when the light turned green. Suddenly, someone caught her attention. Out of the corner of her eye, she saw a man standing at the intersection, and he seemed to be saying something to her. She thought he looked familiar, but when she tried to get a closer look, he had disappeared. Just as the light changed, she saw him again. Rather than move into the intersection, she hesitated a moment. In that moment, a car traveling in the opposite direction ran the light. It would have hit her had she not hesitated. Her miracle of hesitation had possibly saved her life.

Lynn looked again for the man she thought she had seen, but he was nowhere to be found. She thought he might have been an angel, for he had been sent on her behalf to keep her from danger.

Is Lynn one of the blessed ones who really has a guardian angel and did she heed the message his appearance signaled? Why had she wondered who he was and what he was doing in the street? What would have happened had she proceeded without hesitation? Do we, like Lynn, watch for the signs of angels that surround us? Perhaps we should.

Lynn can testify to the fact that her moment of hesitation helped her to avoid an accident. She believes that that hesitation was a miracle. I do too.

Miracles happen every day. Expect yours!

Lord, make us conscious of the angels that surround us and warn us of danger. Help us to realize that they are Your messengers. Amen.

The Miracle of Work

TERRY ENTERED THE CHURCH, looking for the woman he had seen the last time he had come for help. Terry was down on his luck, and he needed financial aid. The woman he sought looked at him and, seeing a healthy, able-bodied man, said, "You need to work; you need a job. Go! Get out of here. Knock on some doors and find yourself a day job. Go!"

No matter how threatening, defiant, and hostile Terry tried to appear, the woman would not be intimidated. She insisted that the church had helped him before, but now it was time for him to help himself. Terry had no choice but to start knocking on some doors.

Not far from the church he found Mrs. White. She needed her grass cut, and she was willing to pay. Terry wanted the job, but he had no tools. What could he use to cut the grass? Out of nowhere a man appeared with all the tools Terry needed. He offered the tools to Terry, who took them and cut Mrs. White's grass.

Terry was paid seventy dollars, and he went back to the church just to say "Thank you" to the woman who had refused to give him a handout. Terry felt good about himself. He had experienced the miracle of work; and he even might have seen an angel bearing tools.

Miracles happen every day. Expect yours!

Lord, make us aware of the opportunities to work. Shake us out of the comfort we often find in accepting handouts rather than stepping out on faith, knowing that You will provide the work we need. Amen.

The Miracle of Generosity

IN JULY 1994, MUCH OF THE STATE of Georgia was flooded by torrential rainfall. Homes, colleges, and businesses all were damaged or destroyed by the floods. There were mass appeals to the government, charities, and individuals to assist in relieving the victims.

Steve owned a sewing business in Georgia. His business was flooded. All of his equipment was destroyed, and his employees were out of work. He did not know what he would do.

Dottie lived in New York. She also operated a sewing business. She heard about Steve. Dottie thought she had some extra equipment that Steve could use, so she decided to get in touch with him. After several attempts, she reached Steve. She told him what she had and that she was willing to give it to him. Steve could not believe her generosity, but he certainly appreciated it.

Steve's wife began to think of Dottie as their guardian angel, but Dottie said that she was only doing what she could to help someone in need. Maybe that is what a guardian angel does.

Miracles happen every day. Expect yours!

Lord, we are often stingy with our resources. Help us to learn the miracle of generosity. Amen.

The Miracle of the Missing Keys

IT WAS JUNE 1991, and Karen was very excited to be cleaning out her desk. She was about to start a new job. As was her custom, she had left her car at the transit station and had taken the train to work. After completing her cleaning tasks, she said good-bye to her co-workers. Upon returning to her car, she discovered that her keys were missing. She tried to remember when she last had had her keys. All she knew was that they had been in her hands when she got out of the car.

She looked around for the transit security office to inquire about lost keys that might have been reported. The transit officer very calmly asked, "Ma'am, have you looked on your windshield?" Karen could not imagine how lost keys could be on her windshield, but she decided to look. And there they were! A young woman, whom Karen calls an angel, had taken her keys out of the door, where Karen had left them in all her excitement, and had informed the security office that she would keep the keys until the end of the day and then leave them on the windshield. This young woman's car recently had been stolen, and she did not want anyone else to experience that kind of heartache.

Karen praises God that her angel found her keys and returned them. Karen's keys were not really missing; they were just in the presence of an angel. It was a miracle.

Miracles happen every day. Expect yours!

Lord, thank You for the many angels You send to save us from our own carelessness. Amen.

The Miracle of Tall Angels

IONA IS A TALL WOMAN, and her son, Shahid, is six feet eight inches tall. He is eighteen years old, and he plays basketball. As a popular high school player, he looked forward to receiving a full basketball scholarship to the college of his choice; however, things just did not work out that way. Iona tried to tell him that he would have to put forth some effort, but he did not believe her. He was arrogant, expecting everything to be handed to him on a silver platter, and he knew that his mother did not know how good he was. But his mother *did* know something, because he graduated from high school without a scholarship. All Iona could do was pray that somehow God would make a way for her son to go to college. She seemed to hear God say, "I have him; he's in My hands."

Shahid's troubles were only beginning. He believed that his mother's household rules were somewhat old-fashioned, and he decided to ignore them. Against his mother's wishes, he listened to X-rated rap music and stayed out late at night, ignoring his curfew. Iona felt that he had chosen to be an adult, so she locked him out of the house. She told him to find a new address and to continue living the type of life he had chosen. Although he knocked on the door for three hours, Iona exercised her own version of tough love and refused to admit him.

Shahid was picked up for shoplifting and stayed in jail ten days. He eventually arranged restitution and was released on probation. Iona prayed all during his incarceration that God would deliver him and make it possible for him to go to college. She heard that same response, "I have him; he's in My hands."

The basketball coach at Knoxville College called to offer Shahid a scholarship. The coach was a tall man and seemed to Iona to be a tall angel. Then one of Iona's tall friends, a missionary, called and said that she was driving to Knoxville and would be happy to take Shahid. She was the second of Iona's tall angels. Iona knew that Shahid would have to report to his probation officer and would have to be under supervision in Knoxville. She discovered that the coach also was a preacher and the sheriff. This tall angel was all things needed. God did have Shahid in His hands, and He sent His tall angels to carry out His miracle.

Miracles happen every day. Expect yours!

Lord, teach us to follow our convictions while listening to Your voice so that we will be obedient in carrying out Your plan for our lives. Amen.

The Miracle of Self-Esteem

PATRICE SUFFERED FROM LOW SELF-ESTEEM. She even says that she hated herself. The only thing that made her feel worthy was the love of men. Having never felt that her father loved her, she wanted some man to love her. She needed a man's love. She offered herself to men, looking for love. She even indulged in drugs with men because she thought that they would love her. Time and again she hit rock bottom, but somehow she bounced back. She was raped and beaten, even left for dead, but she recovered to place herself in the same drug-filled life, looking for love.

During her search for love, she married a man who indulged in drugs with her. The marriage did not last, but it produced a child. Patrice's mother had to care for her child when she was arrested for drug possession and sentenced to jail. Hoping to help Patrice gain some sense of self-esteem, her mother brought her daughter to the jail. The little girl was too young to be allowed inside, but Patrice was allowed to look out of the window at her. When she realized that she could not hold or touch her little girl, she wanted to change her life. Finding a strength she did not know she had, she resolved to make a better life for herself and her daughter.

Eventually Patrice was released from jail, and she discovered that she could write. Writing gave her self-esteem. She felt worthy when she expressed herself on paper. She was hired by the Washington Post because she was a good journalist, and she managed to keep her job—even though it was later discovered that she had lied about her criminal record on her job application. Working as a journalist, she was able to send her daughter to college.

Patrice found the love she had sought in her daughter, whom she called "the love of my life." That love, along with her writing, worked to effect a miracle of self-esteem. Patrice recognized the source of the miracle that changed her life, for she said that God sent an angel to walk beside her and love her.

Miracles happen every day. Expect yours!

Lord, love builds our self-esteem, and with self-esteem we can work miracles. Amen.

The Miracle of Angelic Assistance

IN MARCH 1986, NAT AND ALICE LONG were traveling by car to the Due West United Methodist Church where Nat was scheduled to preach for a revival service. They were accompanied by their friends Blanche and Grady. As they were exiting the expressway, Alice heard a loud crash and felt the impact of a tremendous blow to the rear of the car. As the car in which they were riding was lifted up and spun around, Alice saw a tractor-trailer truck jackknifing and spinning until it lay sideways across the expressway. She knew immediately that the truck had hit them, and she had recovered sufficiently to realize that their car was sliding backward down an embankment.

As they slid down the embankment, Alice noticed that fire followed them, and she realized that the gas tank had been ruptured. The car came to a stop, and Alice knew that they had to get out of the car before it exploded. Flames already had blocked any exit from the right side of the car. The only door that they could open was the driver's. Grady had been driving, and he was the first one out. He helped Alice out. As she exited the car, she was in a near state of panic, for she feared that there was not time to get the two backseat occupants, Nat and Blanche, out.

Suddenly, Alice noticed a woman standing by her side. As Nat lifted Blanche over the front seat, the woman helped Alice pull her out. Nat climbed over the seat, and they all quickly moved what they thought was a safe distance from the car. Within a few minutes, the car and the tires exploded. The woman remained with them and asked if there was anything else she could do. Nat asked her to call the church and tell them that he would not be able to preach for the revival. The woman promised she would, and then she left.

Obviously, the woman called the church, for some of the members met Alice and her party at the police station where they had been taken in a patrol car. As Alice recalls the accident, she feels certain that the woman was an angel sent by God to render assistance. None of the people in the car noticed where the woman came from, if she had a car, or how she got back up the embankment. They just recall that she was extraordinarily calm, purposeful, and efficient in rendering aid. All they know for sure is that she provided angelic assistance as she miraculously worked to save them from a fiery inferno.

Miracles happen every day. Expect yours!

Lord, make us open to the angelic assistance available to us every day. Amen.

The Miracle of Being Grateful

MARIA AND HER SON WERE LEAVING a restaurant when they encountered an elderly, homeless man. His ragged appearance assured them that he was living on the street, and they were moved with compassion. Not only did he appear tired and worn, but he also seemed ill. He walked with a pronounced limp, and he moved slowly and, seemingly, with pain.

In a very feeble voice, the man asked Maria if she could spare any change. Although Maria did not normally give money to people who approached her on the street, there was something about this man that made her want to respond. Maria did not have any change, but she did have some bills. She gave the man five dollars and said, "God bless you."

As she said the words, she realized how blessed she was. She and her son had just left a restaurant. They had been served a delicious meal, but she wondered when that man had last been served in a restaurant. Had he ever even been in one? Suddenly, she was overwhelmingly grateful.

As Maria and her son continued toward their car, she turned to smile at the homeless man and to utter a prayer of thanksgiving. When she turned around, the man had vanished. Only a few seconds had passed, and there was nowhere the man could have gone. The street was not crowded, and it was long and straight. The man should have been clearly in view. His pronounced limp and obvious pain would have prevented him from running fast enough to have been out of sight. He had simply disappeared!

Maria and her son talked about what had just happened. As they discussed the events and the feelings that had come over them, Maria knew that they had been visited by an angel. This angel had brought the message of God's rich and generous blessings to them. They had been reminded of their need to give thanks and to be grateful for their many blessings.

The appearance of the homeless angel was a miracle for Maria. It was a miracle of being grateful.

Miracles happen every day. Expect yours!

Lord, keep us ever mindful of our many blessings. Amen.

The Miracle of Timely Movement

IN JANUARY 1992, MIKE AND HIS FRIENDS attended a back-to-school party. They were all college students and were celebrating the beginning of the spring semester. After thoroughly enjoying being with their friends, they started walking to their car. Their car was parked in a lot across a major intersection, so they decided to race to their car.

Mike remembers hearing police sirens in the distance, but he did not see the cars. Both of his friends had crossed ahead of him. Just as he entered the intersection, he saw a car being chased by a police car. The car was speeding toward him, but he was glued to the spot. The parking lot was dimly lighted, and Mike was not sure if he could be seen. All he knew was that he had to move. But he could not. Both the car being chased and the police car were headed directly toward him.

Mike kept trying to move his feet, but they would not move. He could not remember how to get his legs to go. The cars kept coming. Although Mike knows that only a few seconds passed, he felt as though everything was happening in slow motion. It would take a miracle to save him.

As the cars came within inches of running over him, Mike felt a big hand push him about two feet to the right. The cars rolled smoothly by. Mike's friends witnessed this timely movement from the parking lot. They were relieved that Mike had slid to the right just in the nick of time.

Mike knows that a big hand, an angel, or the will of God moved him. It was a miracle of timely movement.

Miracles happen every day. Expect yours!

Lord, thank You for sending Your angels to watch over us and to move our legs and feet when we fail. We are grateful that You never sleep, leaving us unattended. Amen.

The Miracle of Invisible Cushioning

At the age of two, Skyler was a very active little boy. He was always exploring and getting into mischief. He was especially excited and active on a day when he was attending the birthday party of one of his older friends. Skyler had never been surrounded by so many children engaged in so many different activities.

There were children playing both inside and outside the apartment. Believing Skyler to be absorbed in the inside games, Sky's mother turned her back to assist with some other party matters. Sky heard loud noises from the children outside and ran to the window. As he ran into the window screen, it gave way, and he fell from the second floor window. Sky's mother heard her child's scream and turned around just in time to see him falling. When she got to the open window, she saw her baby's crumpled body on the concrete street below.

Sky was rushed to the hospital emergency room. No one knew what to expect, but his mother kept praying and wondering why she had taken her eyes off him even for a moment. When the examining physician came into the waiting room, he said that there must have been invisible cushioning on that street, for Sky had no broken bones, no internal injuries, and no need for medical treatment. He only had a few scratches. It was a miracle.

Three years later, Sky is still active and healthy. Now his mother has two young boys to keep an eye on. Even as she watches those boys, she remembers Sky's invisible cushioning and thanks God for her miracle.

Miracles happen every day. Expect yours!

Lord, we are so grateful that You never turn away from us. Your protective eye is ever upon us. Thank You. Amen.

The Miracle of Removal

ANNA WORKED AS A HOUSEKEEPER in Guatemala. Her brother always picked her up when her workday was over. He had a beautiful car, and Anna was happy to have such a considerate brother.

One day as they were traveling from work to home, they were forced off the road by a bus, which never stopped to render help. Everything happened so rapidly that Anna was not sure how long they lay trapped in the car. She seemed to drift in and out of consciousness. Each time she awakened, she tried to open the door, but she was unsuccessful. Her brother was never conscious when she was, so she did not know how they would survive.

Then a stranger suddenly appeared and removed her from the car. She kept trying to reach out to the person, but he or she was always out of reach. Within minutes of her removal from the car, her brother was removed. As soon as they safely were placed next to each other on the side of the road, the car in which they had been riding burst into flames. Anna's brother remained unconscious throughout the ordeal. The person or persons who had removed them from the wreckage had disappeared. Anna believes they were angels.

Anna is confident that God sent His angels to save her and her brother, for she knows that it would have taken a miracle to remove them from the type of danger they faced. But Anna believes in miracles.

Miracles happen every day. Expect yours!

Lord, I am expecting my miracle today. It may come in the form of an angel or it may come in another form, but I am ready to receive the blessing it brings. Amen.

The Miracle Cabdriver

IT WAS A COLD DECEMBER MORNING. The temperature had dipped to thirteen degrees, and baby Jay was on his way to the hospital for follow-up surgery. As his parents drove him there, they remembered how Jay had barely survived the first ten months of his life. He had been born with so many defects that the doctors had given him little chance of survival. But survive he had.

Jay was warmly wrapped and tightly held in his mother's arms. She knew that her fragile baby might suffer from the cold temperature, and she was grateful for the warmth of the car. Then the car stopped. Her husband reached for the cellular phone to call for help, but they had forgotten to bring it. Then her husband scribbled "Call 911" on a piece of paper and stood outside the car, holding the sign. Little Jay was still warm, but the car's temperature was rapidly dropping.

Fifteen minutes later, a cab approached and stopped. The cabdriver did not speak English well, but Jay's parents were able to communicate that they needed to get to the hospital immediately. They prayed that this cabdriver would understand as they pointed and directed. They made it in record time.

As Jay's mother rushed into the hospital with him, his father reached for his wallet to pay the cabdriver. But the cabdriver told him in broken English, "God answers prayer. There is no need to pay." Jay's father knew that God had answered his prayer by sending a miracle cabdriver.

Miracles happen every day. Expect yours!

Lord, thank You for miracles that come to us in the form of people who are willing to help in times of need. Amen.

The Christmas Spirit Miracle

TANYA IS CONVINVED that she met a Christmas angel. She says that she and her cousins were waiting to board a rapid-transit train in Berkeley, California, when they were approached by a Native American man who appeared to be slightly intoxicated. They tried not to talk to him, for they had been warned never to talk to strangers. But the man continued to attempt a conversation.

Then a young woman approached the group and asked if anyone could give her a quarter to use the telephone. Both Tanya and her cousins had spent all of their money on gifts and barely had enough for the train; however, the Native American man preceeded to search his pockets for the change. He had pennies, nickels, and dimes—mostly pennies—but he found enough for the phone call. The young woman did not want to take the money, for she felt that it was all the man had. He insisted and said that in the true spirit of Christmas, he wanted to give.

This gesture of kindness opened the lines of communication, and Tanya and her cousins continued to talk to the man. He explained that he was homeless and that because he was usually the one asking, he needed to give. He assigned names to Tanya's cousins, calling them Tinkerbell and Curly, making them laugh. He sat next to them on the train and tried to make everyone talk and laugh.

Soon all of the passengers were smiling and talking to one another. The spirit of Christmas just seemed to take hold of the entire train. Even when the man got off, the spirit he had initiated remained. Tanya is convinced that he was an angel and that the spirit of joy and giving he spread was a miracle.

Miracles happen every day. Expect yours!

Lord, make us ever aware that we may encounter angels in the most unlikely forms and places. Amen.

The Miracle of Safe Return

KIMBERLY WAS DOING SOME Christmas shopping in a crowded mall with her mother and baby sister, Jasmine. Three-year-old Jasmine was tired of her stroller, so she begged her mother to let her get out. Her mother warned her to stay close, but when Jasmine saw Kimberly move away, she tried to follow her.

Missing Jasmine a few minutes later, her mother asked Kimberly if Jasmine was with her. Kimberly replied, "No, isn't she with you?" Then panic set in.

Both mother and daughter started screaming Jasmine's name, but there was no sign of her. How could a little girl disappear so fast?

You can just imagine the many thoughts that flooded their minds. The police were alerted and began to take down Jasmine's description. As they talked with her mother, Kimberly set out on her own search.

Praying as she searched, Kimberly suddenly saw a beautiful woman dressed in gray holding Jasmine's hand. There was a glow about the woman, and Kimberly was sure that she was an angel. Although Jasmine did not run to Kimberly, and Kimberly did not identify herself, the woman smiled and returned Jasmine to her sister. Overcome with relief, Kimberly lifted Jasmine into her arms and turned to thank the woman. She had disappeared! The angel had completed her miracle of safe return.

Kimberly thanked God for the angel and for the miracle.

Miracles happen every day. Expect yours!

Lord, thank You for the angels who help us every day. Amen.

The Miracle of the Deer

SIXTEEN-YEAR-OLD JARRETT EARVIN was driving home in his mother's car when a deer darted out in front of him. Unable to avoid it, he hit the deer. The fatally wounded deer began to fight its attacker, the car. The deer managed to push the car off the road, into a tree and a mailbox, and finally into a ditch. Having subdued its attacker, the deer went to the other side of the road to die.

Miraculously, Jarrett emerged without a scratch from the car, which had been totaled! The neighbor in whose yard he had landed came outside and immediately commented that someone had prayed mightily for him, for there was no way he should have emerged unhurt. Jarrett called his mother with the bad news about her car and the good news about him.

When his mother arrived at the scene of the accident, she started praising God and thanking Him for sending His angel of mercy to protect her son from danger. In the midst of her praising, Jarrett commented, "Mom, I think I saw two deer." His mother responded, "No, son, there was only one deer. The other one was an angel protecting you from harm." It was a miracle, the miracle of the deer.

Miracles happen every day. Expect yours!

Lord, help me to recognize the angels around me in whatever form. They may be bearing my miracle. Amen.

Miraculous Healings

~

The Miracle of Example

ERRI IS AN INTENSIVE CARE NURSE. She has cared for many people who have suffered and died. She also has cared for many who have miraculously lived. After her doctor told her that she would have to have surgery to remove a nodule from her thyroid gland, she wondered whether she would be aligned with those who lived or those who died. You see, the doctor told Terri that the nodule was probably malignant because it secreted fluid that contained malignant cells. In light of these circumstances, the surgery could not wait.

Terri began to pray. She tried to recall the patients she had observed in intensive care. What had been the contributing factors to their death or recovery? Then she remembered the miracle healing she had observed. The thought of this miracle became an example of what was possible through prayer and praise.

One of the patients in Terri's care had been given only a few hours to live. His family was informed, and every family member—twenty in all—assembled at the hospital. The patient's blood pressure had fallen to eighty over sixty, and he was very weak. Nevertheless, the family asked to see him. They all entered his room, carrying a tape recording of their praise songs and ready to take turns in maintaining a constant prayer vigil. They sang and prayed until the dying family member had survived his crisis. The doctor said that what had happened could not be explained; it was simply a miracle.

Now that Terri needed her own miracle, she remembered that family's example. She had seen the power of prayer, and she began to pray. She called her church family and asked them to pray. If that patient had had twenty people praying for him, surely hundreds of people praying for her could not hurt. She went into surgery expecting her miracle, and she found it. The nodule was benign.

Miracles happen every day. Expect yours!

Lord, You have done marvelous things for those who believe. Rid us of our unbelief. Amen.

The Miracle of Time

CAROLYN'S YOUNG FRIEND was a school teacher who genuinely loved children. Although she dreamed of someday having children of her own, after developing several large ovarian tumors, she was told that she would have to have a hysterectomy. If the surgery was performed, her dream of having her own biological children would be lost forever. She saw other doctors, seeking an opinion that would advise against the surgery, but each one she saw offered the surgical solution.

Finally one doctor told her to take her time before undergoing the procedure. He told her that there was no emergency and she should take the time to talk with counselors and pray about the alternatives to having her own children. He told her to think of adoption and to prepare herself both mentally and spiritually for the surgery.

The young teacher took that advice. She prayed and meditated. She asked God to help her bear the cross she had been given. She prayed for the strength to be a mother to the motherless and to be a source of comfort to other women who had undergone hysterectomies. She looked for opportunities to serve God in the new role that He had chosen and not in the role she had chosen for herself.

Feeling spiritually renewed after the time of reflection, she was ready for the surgery. When her doctor examined her before she was to check into the hospital, the tumors had decreased so much in size that the surgery was no longer necessary. It was a miracle, a miracle that had required time.

Miracles happen every day. Expect yours!

Lord, teach us to be patient. Help us take the time to listen to, meditate upon, and prepare to act upon Your word. Amen.

The Miracle of Olympic Gold

I AM SURE THAT WHENEVER ANYONE wins an Olympic gold medal, he or she must believe that a miracle has just taken place. But for Gail Devers, it was an extraordinary miracle. As the gold medal for the one hundred-meter dash was placed around her neck in 1992, she was standing on feet that almost had been amputated a little more than a year before. Those feet that had been swollen and bleeding had made her the fastest woman in the world. It was a miracle!

Gail had been a track star since high school. She excelled in dashes and hurdles. Sometime before the 1988 Olympic games, Gail's health began to fail. She had severe headaches, fainting spells, hair loss, weight fluctuations, brief loss of sight in one eye, loss of sleep, and so much more. It was two years before the correct diagnosis was made. Gail was suffering from a thyroid condition known as Graves' disease. A large cancerous cyst had formed on her thyroid, and immediate treatment was imperative. Conventional treatment involved the use of beta-blockers, which were banned for Olympic competitors, so Gail chose radiation. Although the radiation controlled the thyroid condition, it left her skin so sore that walking made her feet blister, swell, and bleed. A decision was made to amputate both feet. How could she ever compete in the Olympics? It would take a miracle, but Gail believed in miracles. She said, "There is no hurdle too high I can't conquer."

Gail's first miracle saved her feet. Two days before the scheduled amputation, doctors determined that her radiation dosage was too high. Within a month, Gail was walking on feet that were not swollen and bleeding. Within three months, she was winning one hundred-meter hurdle competitions. Within seventeen months, her miracle of Olympic gold became a reality when she completed the one hundred-meter dash in 10.82 seconds at Barcelona, Spain, on August 1, 1992.

Miracles happen every day. Expect yours!

Lord, all things are possible if we believe. Help us daily to run our races and jump our hurdles, winning gold medals for our faith. Amen.

The Miracle of Healing Hands

CATHERINE'S SON, RYAN, WAS BORN with extensive muscle deprivation and partial paralysis. She was told that if her child ever learned to feed himself, she could consider herself blessed. Catherine could not imagine life with a child for whom the most she could hope was the ability to feed himself. She knew somehow that God intended more for her and for Ryan.

Catherine consulted several medical doctors. They all stressed that a major goal for Ryan would be to learn to feed himself. Then Catherine decided to hope for a miracle. She left the conventional medical field and took her thirteen-month-old son to a spiritual healer. She was convinced that such a person would not hurt her son, and she hoped that maybe a healer could help.

She selected a spiritual healer named Joann. Joann claimed the gift of healing, and Catherine asked her to heal Ryan. Joann prayed for Ryan and placed him on her healing table. The undeveloped muscles in Ryan's body felt like mush under Joann's hands, but as she stroked them and prayed, they took on new form. Ryan started to do things that physically he had been unable to do. He sat up, waved his hand, and watched the skin that covered the paralyzed lower half of his body take on new shape under Joann's healing touch.

Today Ryan does more than feed himself; he walks, rides his bike, talks, and functions as other children his age. Catherine knows that Joann's healing hands effected a miracle.

Miracles happen every day. Expect yours!

Lord, we are so quick to accept the ordinary and doubt the extraordinary. You are every-where, performing miracles for those who believe. Amen.

The Miracle of the Coat Hanger

PAULA DIXON HAD BEEN INVOLVED in a motorcycle accident, but she was on her way to Hong Kong from London and felt well enough to travel. When she boarded the airplane, the cabin crew noticed her bruised arm and her discomfort in moving. (She had fractured two to four ribs.) The crew could not see that her lung was collapsing, but they did notice her difficulty in breathing. Paula was made as comfortable as possible, and the plane took off. Once airborne, Paula's breathing worsened, and professional help was sought.

Professor Angus Wallace, an orthopedic surgeon, happened to be aboard. His very presence on the plane was the first miracle. He knew that something would have to be done to assist Paula. Even attempting to land the plane might cause her breathing to worsen due to pressure changes. He needed to insert a tube so that the trapped air could escape, relieving her breathing.

Ingeniously using a coat hanger, bottled water, plastic serving knives and forks, and Scotch tape, Professor Wallace constructed the necessary tubing. The procedure was painful, and the only anesthetic available was brandy. Miraculously, the makeshift contraption worked, the air escaped, and Paula was able to withstand the landing without incident. She was taken to a London hospital, treated, and released.

Both the attending physicians at the hospital and the passengers aboard the airplane were certain that Professor Wallace had performed a miracle. And I agree.

Miracles happen every day. Expect yours!

Lord, thank You for professionals who are ready to use their skills to help others. Amen.

The Miracle of the Wildflower

FOR THREE YEARS, JACLYN BUCKLEY suffered with leukemia. Although having this disease was especially tough on a child who was only three years old when diagnosed, today she is in remission and has an excellent chance of living a long and fruitful life. What happened to Jaclyn might be classified as an everyday miracle of nature.

An extract from a rare wildflower, a rosy periwinkle plant, proved to be a cancer-fighting medicine. This plant, which was first discovered in Madagascar, is one of many endangered plant and animal species. It produces vincristine, which is used as a major treatment for leukemia, especially among children. This wildflower extract was used from the start in treating Jaclyn. Her pediatrician says that the medicinal value of plants is extraordinary.

God has provided many miracles for us in nature. Nearly one-fourth of all prescriptions written in the United States today are based on substances derived from natural products, and only about five percent of them have been studied.

Jaclyn has appeared as the poster child for the Endangered Species Coalition and once appealed to Interior Secretary Bruce Babbitt to save the Endangered Species Act, which might protect other life-saving species.

Sometimes our own insensitivity works against the everyday miracles God has in store for us. I am glad that Jaclyn's pediatrician was sensitive to the miracle in store for her.

Miracles happen every day. Expect yours!

Lord, make us sensitive to our destruction of the many varieties of plants and animals You have created. Many of them are Your miracle agents. Amen.

The Miracle of Biological Relationship

THE CLACK FAMILY WAS TOLD that their adopted daughter, Alicia, suffered from aplastic anemia, a disease that prohibits the body from producing red and white blood cells and platelets. A bone-marrow transplant was needed to save her. Knowing that the best donors would be those with a biological relationship, specifically siblings, the Clacks first had Alicia's biological brother, whom they also had adopted, tested. His bone marrow did not match. Then the Clacks embarked upon the discovery of their daughter's other siblings and prayed for a miracle.

Their first challenge was to convince a judge to unseal Alicia's adoption records. They met that challenge, and they located two older sisters whom Alicia never knew existed. Both of them matched, so they had two chances of saving their daughter. They came to a new realization that biological relationship is a miracle. God carefully matches even the bone marrow of some relatives.

Both of Alicia's sisters agreed to the transplant, and the doctors decided which would be the better donor. The procedure was smooth, and the donor sister was out of the hospital shopping for a birthday present for her newly discovered sister the very next day. Alicia celebrated her thirteenth birthday during her nineteen-day hospital stay.

Alicia is recovering. She is learning to draw her own blood, change her dressings, and take her medication without assistance. She takes walks with her mother in an effort to regain her strength, and she and her siblings plan to promote the need for bone-marrow donors. They want others to have the opportunity to experience the miracle they have shared.

Miracles happen every day. Expect yours!

Lord, thank You for biological relationships and for relatives who are willing to share not only their material possessions but also their very bodies. Jesus set the example; help us to learn from Him. Amen.

The Miracle of Loving Support

ONE YEAR AGO, SUZY FOUND OUT that she had breast cancer. Of course, the news was devastating. She prayed for the strength to face the operations, chemotherapy, and radiation that she was told awaited her. As the months progressed, she had several operations and painful sessions of chemotherapy and radiation. She experienced all the negative effects. She lost her hair, she could not eat, and she felt unattractive. Then she experienced the miracle of loving support.

Suzy's doctors and nurses never stopped showing loving concern while providing excellent medical care. They took the time to encourage her, show her how to take her medication, and help her with her therapy. They actually believed she would make it. She felt their loving support.

Then there were her co-workers. They helped her believe in her attractiveness even while she lost her hair. They helped her believe in herself. They showed love and concern when she was too sick to come to work, and they visited her at home and in the hospital. They helped her experience her miracle.

And there were her pets. Both Suzy's dog and horse gave her unconditional love. She felt that she had to live in order to return that love. They were her special medicine, for even animals help to work miracles of love and support.

Miracles happen every day. Expect yours!

Lord, thank You for the love and support that bring healing with their special kind of medicine. Amen.

The Miracle of Self-Cure

DR. ROSENBERG HAS BEEN RESEARCHING the ability of the human body to cure itself of various illnesses. He has been especially intrigued by a sixty-three-year-old man who came to see him needing gallbladder surgery.

While taking this patient's medical history, Dr. Rosenberg discovered that the man had been diagnosed with cancerous tumors on his stomach and liver. He had undergone surgery, but his doctors had informed him that they could not remove all of the malignancies, and he was sent home to die. The shocking revelation was that the diagnosis and surgery had taken place twelve years before. How could this man still be alive? Had he been misdiagnosed? Had he been miraculously cured? Was the currently needed gallbladder surgery even possible?

Dr. Rosenberg continued to carefully take the patient's history, examine him, and document his findings. Convinced that the patient's current complaint of abdominal pain was caused by the gallbladder, Dr. Rosenberg proceeded with the surgery. Expecting to find numerous tumors in the abdominal cavity, he was shocked when he found none. He could only surmise that the man's body had cured itself.

This miraculous self-cure was no surprise to the patient. He had decided not to die twelve years ago, and he had expected the miracle that had become a reality.

Miracles happen every day. Expect yours!

Lord, You have wondrously made our bodies capable of self-cure. Help us to believe in that ability as You work Your miraculous healing power. Amen.

The Miracle of the Healing Circle

In 1985, Niro was sick. She had diarrhea, sweats, aches, pain, and weakness. She did not understand what was happening to her. The doctors told her that she had AIDS-Related Complex. She was HIV positive. How could that be? She did not believe that heterosexual women who had not been drug users or had blood transfusions could be HIV positive. When her lover died of AIDS, she discovered that he had been bisexual.

Niro refused to believe that she would develop AIDS. She believed in miracles, and she decided to expect one. There had to be something she could do. She began with daily meditation. She walked the beaches near her home at 5:30 A.M., meditating on her cure, her miracle. She believed that meditation would be a key element. Because she is a therapist, she decided to bring others with a similar diagnosis into a "healing circle." Together they would meditate on positive thoughts and share good health news.

Niro decided to take no medicines. If she expected her miracle, she had to act in faith. She ate only natural foods, concentrated on her meditating, and used imagery to visualize a body free of the virus that had weakened her.

Today she travels the world with her message of how her diagnosis was an awakening to personal enlightenment. There is no evidence in her blood that Niro was ever HIV positive. the miracle of her healing circle has become a reality.

Miracles happen every day. Expect yours!

Lord, help us to live the kind of lives that are centered on positive thoughts, sensible diets, and service and devotion to You. Amen.

The Flat-Line Miracle

IN 1989, JOE'S HEART was so greatly enlarged and damaged that the doctors predicted he would be dead within a year if he didn't retire and get plenty of rest. Surgery was not practical because of the extensive damage to his heart, so Joe had no choice but to follow the doctors' orders. He retired, rested, and did something the doctors did not mention—he prayed.

Joe and his wife, Dora, engaged in hours, days, and years of prayer. They read meditations together, and they believed in miracles as they constantly asked God for one. Surely the God who had made Joe's heart could return it to its normal size. By 1994, Joe was off medication, his heart had returned to its normal size, and it was functioning without complications.

But in January 1995, Joe suffered a heart attack. He needed bypass surgery. Dora, a registered nurse, rushed Joe to the hospital and understood the full meaning of the doctor's diagnosis of a right-side blockage. Dora prayed even as she assisted the doctor in administering morphine for the tremendous pain that Joe felt. Joe drifted in and out of consciousness and complained of being cold.

Joe recalls those moments. He says that the type of cold he felt was penetrating. He had never felt so cold in his life. Then, suddenly, he felt warm. There was no pain; he was at peace. It was at that time that he had flat-lined. His heart had stopped.

Dora saw the flat-line. She prayed out loud, "Don't you leave me now! Oh, God, don't let him leave me now!" Because of his past heart history, and because of the seemingly miraculous recovery in which the doctors had neither participated nor believed, the medical staff was ready to pull the sheet over Joe's head. But Dora kept on praying, and that flat-line ceased being flat. Joe's heart had started beating again. It was a miracle, and Joe has lived to tell about it!

Miracles happen every day. Expect yours!

Lord, don't let us give up while You're still working. Amen.

The Miracle of Nutrition

HEPHZIBAH HAD ALWAYS BEEN an advocate of exercise. Even in her native Sri Lanka, she had walked many miles daily. She also felt that she maintained a healthy, nutritious diet, so when the oncologist told her that she had advanced stages of breast cancer, she could not believe it. The oncologist, well respected in his field, advised her to have the breast removed immediately. Hephzibah would not hear of it. She just believed that God intended for her to live and die with both of her breasts.

She decided to visit a nutrition specialist, believing that he could recommend a diet that would put the cancer in remission. Neither her husband nor her son agreed with her decision, but Hephzibah was determined. After confirming the advanced stage of the cancer, the nutritionist recommended a program of exercise and diet that included fruits, vegetables, and, occasionally, a small portion of fish—but no meat. Her family felt this diet would not work and pleaded with Hephzibah to go ahead with the surgery. Although they tried to convince her that she was playing with her life, Hephzibah insisted that she had faith in God's intention to cure her, and she believed the diet would be His vehicle.

Hephzibah's son, Paul, was very troubled by his mother's actions. He could not accept her decision, but he knew of her great faith. He asked God to show him some sign that his mother was doing the right thing. A few days later, Paul was browsing in a bookstore. He picked up a book on cancer and opened it. On the page in front of him was the name of a nutritionist who was making remarkable strides in curing cancer through diet. It was the nutritionist his mother was seeing! Paul thanked God for showing him that sign. He was convinced that his mother was following the will of God and would be cured without the surgery she so adamantly opposed.

Within months, the cancer had shrunk. Within two years, the nutritionist found no sign that there ever had been a cancer. Hephzibah returned to the oncologist for confirmation that the cancer had disappeared. He gave her the confirmation and labeled its disappearance a miracle. Hephzibah had already labeled her cure a miracle of nutrition.

Miracles happen every day. Expect yours!

Lord, thank You for food that heals us and for the faith to submit to Your will for our lives. Amen.

The Miracle Healing

EIGHTEEN-MONTH-OLD LINDSAY was very sick. She had none of her usual spunk and sparkle. In fact, she had not had anything to eat or drink for thirty-six hours. She had not even gone to the bathroom. It seemed as though her bodily functions had shut down.

Her mother and father were very worried. What had happened to their happy child? She was burning up with fever, perspiring, and agonizing in pain. She had not moved from her bed for hours. It was serious. Her parents decided that they had done all the pleading and coaxing possible, but Lindsay just was not responding. The hospital was the next step.

While her mother called the doctor and asked him to meet them at the hospital, her father started praying. He prayed in the most earnest and sincere manner possible. He stayed on his knees, begging Jesus to heal his baby. He believed that Jesus had the power to heal, and he knew that Jesus loved and had healed children while on earth. He finally proclaimed, "In the name of Jesus, be healed!"

When he opened his eyes, Lindsay was smiling. She had not smiled in thirty-six hours, but she was smiling. He felt her forehead, and it was cool. The fever had broken. She sat up, hopped off the bed, and started toward the kitchen, where her mother was trying to reach the doctor.

Lindsay told her mother that she wanted to eat and drink. Her mother told the doctor that she did not think she would need him. She hung up the phone and hugged and fed her child.

Lindsay's father had been so overcome with emotion upon seeing his child cured in the twinkling of an eye that he had fallen to his knees, crying and thanking God for the miraculous cure. Although he had prayed for the miracle healing, he had been shocked when it had occurred. He promised to tell their miracle story everywhere, and he would not forget to give God thanks and praise.

Miracles happen every day. Expect yours!

Lord, thank You for miraculous cures. Help us to recognize them when they occur and be ready to give You the praise! Amen.

The Miracle of Sight

It was a beautiful spring Sunday, and Dot was outside playing with her friends. They were having a wonderful time and could not understand why some of the neighborhood boys started throwing rocks. One of the rocks hit Dot in the right eye. She fell to the ground. When she got up, her face was covered in blood and she could not see.

Dot ran around in circles, crying for her mother, but she could not see how to get to her. Then she heard her mother's voice, asking what had happened, and she moved in the direction of that voice. As her mother wiped away the blood and tried to stop the swelling with ice packs, Dot kept crying that she could see only darkness, and she confessed that she was afraid.

The neighbors joined her mother, forming a prayer circle around her. They held their Bibles and prayed that God would restore Dot's sight. While they were praying, Dot began to see light, but everything was blurred and she was in extreme pain.

Ignoring Dot's pain and swollen face, her mother took her to church for the evening service and asked the church to pray for her child.

Slowly the swelling subsided, and Dot's eyesight was restored. It was a miracle; but on the heels of that miracle, Dot suffered a stroke on the right side of her face. The stroke was an aftereffect of the injury to the eye, and it left her mouth twisted to one side.

The children made fun of Dot, calling her "a one-eyed monster." But Dot decided to use the weapon her mother had used to restore her sight. She prayed. From the time school was out in the summer until it started again in the fall, Dot prayed that her face would return to normal and the children would stop calling her names.

When the first day of school arrived, Dot's face was back to normal. It was a miracle!

Miracles happen every day. Expect yours!

Lord, teach us to believe in miracles! Amen.

The Miracle of Blood

WITHOUT KNOWING IT, my husband had been bleeding internally for several days. When his strength had failed to the point that he could not change a lightbulb without tiring, he knew it was time to seek help. I prayed every step of the way to the doctor's office, hoping that this six-foot-five-inch, two hundred and forty-pound man would not pass out before I got him there. We barely made it.

When the nurses had taken his blood count, they told me that he had lost half the blood in his body and had to be hospitalized immediately for blood transfusions. They said, "He is half dead!" My husband looked at them and said, "I am half alive!"

By the time I had completed the admission process, the life-giving units of blood had been ordered and were being administered. Even though the doctor admitted that, in spite of screening, there is the possibility of receiving tainted blood, blood replacement was his only hope for holding on to the half of life he so boldly claimed.

The blood, along with the prayers of the saints, performed its miracle. It gave my husband back the other half of his life without surgery. Blood is a lifegiving, miraculous gift of God. Its very presence performs miracles consistently.

Miracles happen every day. Expect yours!

Lord, thank You for the blood that even now flows through our veins, giving us life. Amen.

The Miracle of Resolve

IN 1982, FRED WAS DIAGNOSED as having epilepsy. He had seizures and was given the medication Dilantin. Fred took his medication every day, for he wanted to avoid the unpleasant experience of having a seizure. Sometimes he could feel a seizure coming on, so he would double his doses of Dilantin.

Then one day, after having taken Dilantin for six years, Fred decided that he did not want to be a slave to medication. He decided to pray that God would deliver him from his sickness. He knew that God could, but he wondered if God would. Was his wish God's will? What if he had a seizure so severe that it killed him? How would his family ever understand that his stubbornness and refusal to take his medication had killed him? What should he do?

Fred prayed for guidance, and hearing his answer deep within, he resolved not to take the medicine again. He knew that God not only *could* but also *would* deliver him, and he decided to commit himself to the work of kingdom building.

Four years later, Fred is still seizure-free, and he is studying to be a minister. His resolve delivered him. He experienced a miracle.

Miracles happen every day. Expect yours!

Lord, help us to remember that if we pray and do not doubt, we can and will experience miracles. Amen.

The Miracle of Relief

GAYLE WAS DIAGNOSED with ulcerated colitis in 1978. Surgery was performed, and after her one-month hospital stay, she was told that she would have to wear a bag for the rest of her life. Gayle was devastated. She was only twenty-one years old, and she could not imagine going through life with a bag. How would she date? How would she ever have self-confidence? Why had this happened to her?

Her state of mind, the worry, and the questions took their toll. In 1979, additional surgery was required to remove more of her colon. Gayle was seriously ill. She says that she was literally knocking at death's door. She knew that she needed help from God.

Gayle became a praying person. She asked God to reveal His will for her life. She prayed for strength to survive all that she had to bear, and she prayed that somehow the bag could be removed. It would be such a relief not to have to wear the bag. She wanted a miracle of relief.

Slowly, Gayle began to feel better—even with the bag and in spite of the fact that she weighed only ninety-seven pounds. She was extremely busy, working and attending school full time. Something within, a hope that would not be denied, told her that she would be delivered from the bag. She would get her miracle of relief.

Gayle joined a support group for others with similar illnesses. She was encouraged to accept life with the bag. She was shown how to wear the type of clothes that concealed the bag. She enrolled in a modeling class to build her self-confidence and self-esteem. She began to gain weight, even to play tennis, but she had to wear that dreaded bag.

Thirteen years passed, and there was no miracle. Then in October 1991, Gayle saw an article in the Sunday news magazine. She read of a new surgery for people like her. An 800 number was given to call for references and testimonials from those who had undergone the surgery and been relieved of their bags. Gayle called immediately. She talked to one woman who had had the surgery, and she knew that this was her miracle, the answer to her prayers.

Gayle traveled to St. Petersburg, Florida, for the surgery, and on November 25, 1991, she had the operation. She was hospitalized for twenty-one days, and her insurance paid every cent. She experienced no pain after the successful surgery. Her doctor was amazed by her wonderful recovery, but she knew that her Bible class was praying for her.

Gayle felt in her heart that it was not God's will for her to wear a bag for the rest of her life. She never gave up hope that her miracle of relief would come, and she was ready for it when it came. She says that it was all in the plan, in divine order. She knew that her miracle of relief came from God.

Miracles happen every day. Expect yours!

Lord, teach us patience and readiness to accept Your will for our lives. If we are faithful, we will be blessed. Amen.

The Miracle of Learning to Love

IN 1984, MICHAEL WAS TOLD that he had six months to live. He was an alcoholic, and he had AIDS. He felt despair because his father had wished the dreaded disease on him, his homosexual son. Michael could not help wondering if his father's wish had caused his affliction. Logically, he knew he had acquired it through sexual promiscuity.

Michael decided that he could wish for a miracle. He believed in a higher power, and he knew that he could begin a spiritual journey that would result in wholeness. This would be his miracle.

He started attending Alcoholics Anonymous meetings at 7:30 A.M. before going to work. As a floral designer, he found that he was enjoying his work more being sober. Then Mike had to make a decision about medication. He decided not to take AZT, the most popular drug for his condition. But he did decide to try MAC, Mycobacterium Avium Complex, which can have sickening side effects but which he believed in. He also used a drug that triggers immune cell activity.

But Michael says that what really has worked to keep him from death—as was predicted—was learning how to love another human being unconditionally. Learning to love unconditionally is in itself a miracle.

Miracles happen every day. Expect yours!

Lord, teach us to love one another. Amen.

The Miracle of the Comeback Kid

IT HAD BEEN A YEAR since Kimberly was caught in crossfire among five men involved in an argument over a woman. Kimberly was hit in her face, and she still carries a small scar, but the important thing is that she is alive and well.

At the time of her injury, Kimberly had been playing with two friends near her home. She could not understand what had happened to her. She had always believed that her neighborhood was safe. She never expected to suffer a gunshot wound. But she was seriously hurt, and she was very frightened. It would take more than surgery and healing to make her well again. She would have to learn to trust people again. She would have to learn again to play in her neighborhood without fear. That would be a tall order for an eight-year-old.

But as the year passed, Kimberly made a miraculous comeback. Her grandmother is an assistant pastor at the church they attend, and with love and prayers Kimberly has recovered.

Kimberly sings in the church choir, and one Sunday the mayor came to hear her sing a solo. He had taken a personal interest in Kimberly because he has a daughter her age, and he knows that his daughter could have been caught in just such a crossfire.

Kimberly does not have to worry anymore about a safe place to play, for the city has opened youth centers near her home and around other housing projects. The mayor has even taken Kimberly and her friends out for pizza. He tells her that he is proud of her and that he wants their city to be safe for all children.

She has made a miraculous comeback, and her brush with death has resulted in improvements for all the children of her city. She and her grandmother are grateful to God for sparing her life. They count it a miracle!

Miracles happen every day. Expect yours!

Lord, protect our children as they play, and help us to keep their neighborhoods safe. Amen.

The Miracle of a Heart

CHESTER SZUBER HAD BEEN ON THE WAITING LIST for a new heart for four and a half years. He was growing weaker and tired easily. He often wondered how long he would be able to survive. His seventeen-year-old daughter, Patty, had decided four years ago to be an organ donor. She knew how difficult it was for people like her father to find good organs, and she wanted to help someone in need if the opportunity arose.

Then the unthinkable happened. Patty was killed in an automobile accident caused by a drunk driver. All of her organs were made available for those on the waiting lists. The doctors informed Chester that his daughter's heart was a match for him. He immediately refused, for he could not imagine using his daughter's heart. He was grieving for his daughter. Though he was making arrangements for her kidneys to give better quality life to two waiting recipients and her eyes to give sight to two blind recipients, he could not agree to have her heart improve the quality of his own life.

He decided to talk it over with the other members of his family. At first his wife refused to consider it, thinking that she would lose him as well as her daughter. But then all decided that it was what Patty would have wanted.

The operation was successfully performed, and Chester was given his daughter's heart. The fact that his daughter had agreed to be an organ donor and the fact that her heart perfectly matched her father's need was a miracle. As the family said, "Patty is gone, but not dead. She lives in all of the people with whom she shared her organs and tissue."

Even out of tragedy, miracles can happen.

Miracles happen every day. Expect yours!

Lord, teach us to be willing to share ourselves with others. Your Son gave His life. We can give our organs. Amen.

The Miracle of the
Missed Date with Death

CRISTOFER'S DOCTORS TOLD HIM that he would be lucky to be alive in eighteen months. He had a definite date with death. He was warned that he would become progressively weaker and that soon he would not have the strength to snap a matchstick. You see, Cristofer was diagnosed with AIDS.

But, miraculously, Cristofer has missed his date with death. In fact, he has missed that date by ten years! Cristofer is still alive, and he can do more than snap a matchstick. Daily he hauls cement blocks as he builds retaining walls for the terraces around his home. He engages in this strenuous, demanding work of hauling these blocks by hand, and he says that he feels better physically than he has ever felt in his life.

What happened to his date with death? No one really knows. Cris is categorized as a "long-term AIDS survivor." This means that he is among that group of AIDS patients who have lived at least three years after a diagnosis of AIDS. Cris has watched his friends die of the disease, and he often feels lonely. The way he combats that loneliness may very well be a clue to his miracle of survival.

Cris has changed his eating habits to a modest, sensible diet, and he spends his time working hard and talking to young people about the dangers of unprotected sex. He enthusiastically works to maintain his hillside home and gardens and refuses to prepare to die. Has he positively worked to miss his date with death, or was it a miracle? Is there any difference?

Miracles happen every day. Expect yours!

Lord, help us to live positive, wholesome lives. Teach us to eat sensibly, work hard, and give unselfishly in service to others. Amen.

The Miracle of Resurrection

JACK AND JUSTINE HAD BEEN MARRIED for many years, but for the past several years, Jack had been very ill. Justine never tired of caring for him. No matter what the need, if she could, she provided. She often prayed that God would give her the strength to endure and that Jack's physical body would survive all infirmities.

One day Justine was bathing Jack. He slumped over, lost control of his bodily functions, and died. Justine knew he was dead, but she could not face it. She started praying that God would resurrect him. She told God that she could not look at her dead husband, she could not call the ambulance, she could not do anything at all.

Justine heard a loud voice that said, "Things are not as they appear. All sickness is not unto death." Justine ran to get her Bible. She was directed to John 11, the story of Lazarus. Just as Mary and Martha had believed about their brother, Justine believed that her husband would live again in the resurrection. Her eyes fell on verse 40: "But didn't I tell you that you will see a wonderful miracle from God if you believe?" (TLB). Justine responded, "I believe, but I just can't look at Jack."

Then Justine placed Jack's head on her shoulder, allowing him to lean on her. She felt the full weight of his dead body, but she did not look at him. Then she started reciting the Twenty-third Psalm. As she said each verse, she kept believing in the resurrection. Near the end of the Psalm, Jack lifted his head and said, "I left you for a little while, didn't I?"

Jack lived for eighteen more years. Justine had her resurrection miracle!

Miracles happen every day. Expect yours!

Lord, we believe. Help our unbelief. Amen.

Miraculous Rescues

The Miracle of a Whimper

NE FRIDAY AFTERNOON, while hiking with her father and siblings in the Chattahoochee National Forest, two-year-old Naomi disappeared. By Saturday morning, more than two hundred volunteers were searching through the cold, dark woods, hoping to find her. The searchers wondered how she could have vanished and how they would ever find her. Two years old is so young. They could only imagine how frightened she might be, and they knew that it would take a miracle to find her alive and unharmed.

Rescue worker Kip Clayton used a computer program to help him in the search. The program was new but remarkable, helping to guide him in his search. He could not bear the thought of one more child lost and found murdered, and he was determined to find Naomi. He just kept using his program and praying for a miracle.

By Saturday afternoon, the rescue workers were fearing the worst. How could that baby survive? But Kip kept using his program to guide him. He found Naomi lying face down beside a log. When he saw her blue and bloated body, he thought she was dead. He was afraid to touch her, believing that there had been foul play. He did not want to disturb any evidence.

Then came the miracle of a whimper. Naomi whimpered, and Kip picked up the cold, frightened, wet child, holding her close in his arms. God had led him to her; she was safe. It was a miracle! He wept in humble thanksgiving.

By Saturday night, Naomi was in the hospital recovering from exposure, watching television, and smiling, surrounded by her family. They were so glad she had been able to whimper. That whimper was a miracle!

Miracles happen every day. Expect yours!

Lord, thank You for computer programs and dedicated rescue workers. They work with You to effect miracles. Amen.

The Miracle of Human Instinct

WHEN WE READ IN THE NEWS about brutal murders and mothers killing their children, we might wonder whether our basic human nature causes us to be selfish and uncaring. But let me tell you about a miracle that was sparked by human instinct, the kind of basic instinct that causes us to be unselfish and unbelievably brave.

Brian Bennett was gathering his gear after an afternoon of fishing and relaxing, when he saw a car slowly rolling into the lake and heard a father frantically screaming that his children were inside. The father was even trying to hold the car, but he was not strong enough.

Acting on human instinct, Brian shed his shoes, shirt, and socks and dove into the lake to try to save the children. Brian tried to open the car door and pull the children out before it completely submerged, but he could not do it. As the car rapidly filled with water, he was able to get the door open. Miraculously, one of the children was near the door, and Brian grabbed that child and kept fanning the water and feeling for the other child. Both of the children, ages one and three, were struggling because they were so frightened. This made it more difficult for Brian to swim to the surface, holding the children out of the water as he backstroked toward shore.

Neither of the children's parents could swim, so they prayed as Brian worked to rescue their children. Other fishermen assembled to help pull Brain and the children out of the water. Brian was completely exhausted when he was pulled ashore. One observer commented, "I don't think he realized the extent of what he did. He just swam out there and got the kids, no questions asked." He had truly become a "fisher of people."

Brian, the father of two young sons of his own, said, "I think anybody would have done it, like I hope they would for my kids." He said that he acted on instinct and that God had given him miraculous strength. When the parents tried to thank him, he told them, "You can thank the Lord." Those parents did thank the Lord for Brian, for their children, and for the human instinct that caused Brian to unselfishly risk his own life to save others. It was a miracle.

Miracles happen every day. Expect yours!

Lord, thank You for the goodness of human instinct. Help more of us to experience it every day. Amen.

The Miracle of Patience

JAMIE PEAVY LEARNED THE MIRACLE of patience the hard way. She was traveling to visit a friend when she ran off the road in her pickup truck just one mile from the Dallas-Fort Worth International Airport. She had to wait patiently for two and one-half days for a miracle. There was no one around. Who would find her pinned in her truck, unable to move her legs or open the door?

It was a miracle that Jamie remained conscious and was able to ration the few mints she had and hang her purse out the window to scoop water from the creek below. She had to learn the miracle of patience. Just in case no one found her, she decided to write a note to her family. Using her lipstick, she explained that no one had killed her and that she was pinned in after having run off the road. She closed her note by telling her family that she loved them. Satisfied that she could do no more, she began her wait. Her miracle of patience took over.

Two and one-half days later, a construction worker who was inspecting a site near the airport discovered her. She had suffered two broken legs, a broken wrist, a broken rib, a punctured lung, cuts, bruises, and dehydration. But her miracle of patience had kept her alive!

Miracles happen every day. Expect yours!

Lord, when there is nothing else I can do, teach me to patiently wait for You. Amen.

The Miracle of the Tear

DEBRA'S FATHER WAS A MORTICIAN, and she was accustomed to passing bodies in the mortuary as she arrived home from school. A new body had just arrived, and Debra looked to see if she knew who it was.

The body covering had been removed, for the embalming process was soon to begin. Debra looked at the body. There was something different about the face, but she could not decide what it was. She studied the face again. Then she saw it. There was a tear coming out of one of the man's eyes. He was crying! But dead men don't cry, do they?

Debra ran to find her father. She reported what she had seen, and her father verified it. Upon further examination, it was discovered that the man was not dead at all. The tear had saved his life. It was a miracle.

Miracles happen every day. Expect yours!

Lord, we are often quick to assume the worst. Give us the patience we need as we hope for the best. Amen.

The Miracle of Coincidence

IN MARCH 1992, KENDRA BOARDED a flight from New York to Cleveland. She was leaving a successful sales conference, and she felt quite proud of her accomplishments. In fact, she was in such a good mood that she neither complained about having to wait while the plane was being deiced nor about discovering that someone else was sitting in her assigned seat. She just moved to an unoccupied one.

She was somewhat nervous about flying in such snowy weather, and the seat to which she had moved was next to the window, which she found to be unsettling. The person next to her noticed her distress and asked if she would prefer the aisle seat. She did, and once again she changed seats.

The plane had to be deiced again and was delayed another thirty minutes. Finally, they took off. Almost immediately there was trouble. The ice on the wings caused the plane to tilt, flip over, and crash into Flushing Bay, breaking into three pieces. Kendra remembers being thrown outside the plane and then regaining consciousness, still strapped in her seat and floating in frigid water. She saw smoke and fire everywhere, and she was experiencing terrible pain.

She tried to block out the pain and concentrate on freeing herself from the seatbelt and climbing out of the water to shore. The water in which she had landed was only four feet deep, and later she would wonder if that wasn't one of the miracles of coincidence that surrounded her survival.

Kendra finally saw a man in the distance. She managed to reach him, and he offered words of comfort and provided the help she needed. Kendra's injuries were critical. She had crushed ribs, a punctured lung, lung damage from smoke inhalation, and severe burns on most of her body. How had she survived? It must have been a miracle.

Then Kendra discovered the coincidences that made her survival even more miraculous. Of the fifty-one passengers on board, twenty-seven had been killed. Among the twenty-seven were both the person who had taken her assigned seat and the person with whom she had switched seats. Was it a miracle of coincidence, or was it just a miracle?

Kendra knows that she survived for a purpose, and she has become a part of the U.S. Air Disaster Coalition, a group of survivors and families of air disasters. This group is a source of mutual support and lobbies for safe flight reform.

Kendra is more appreciative of all of life and thanks God for the miracle of coincidence that saved her life.

Miracles happen every day. Expect yours!

Lord, thank You for the millions of safe flights that take place every day. Make us more careful of all that we can do to prevent flight disasters. Amen.

The Miracle Lake

HAROLD HAD DECIDED TO GO HUNTING. Although he told his wife that he was going, he did not tell her where he was going. He also failed to tell her when he would return. None of these facts seemed important until he became ill. When he reached the hunting stand, he almost did not climb into it because he was feeling so ill; but he thought that if he rested for a while, he would be able to enjoy his outing.

Once in the stand, his sickness escalated. He started vomiting and lost consciousness. While unconscious, he fell out of the stand onto the ground below. When he regained consciousness, he realized that both his hip and shoulder were either broken or out of place. His shoulder was movable, and he could hear bones crushing.

Realizing that he was cold, he thought of his backpack. He could see it, along with his gun, on a rack in the hunting stand. He could not reach it or even raise himself up from the ground. His pack also contained the juices, food, and blanket he so desperately needed to survive.

Then Harold started to pray. He had to make peace with God, for he did not believe he would ever be found. Death appeared to be imminent.

Harold prayed all night long. At one point he heard some shots and shouted for help, but no one heard him. Then he heard some dogs growling and feared they would attack him, but, miraculously, they ran away when he yelled at them.

Harold was still sick and vomiting. He suspected food poisoning. Dehydration was taking over. Harold knew that he had to get some water from somewhere. He managed to twist himself around on a log and noticed that there was a lake about one hundred yards away. He began dragging himself toward the lake. Occasionally, he stopped to eat a bit of tree bark or an earthworm or lice. He even found a discarded Pepsi can about a third full of rainwater, and he quickly drank it. It took him a day and a night, but he finally made it to the lake. He used the can as his glass to drink from the lake. He knew that the lake was his miracle and perhaps would save his life. It had been two days since he had fallen from the hunting stand.

Harold's wife sensed that something was wrong. Although he had not told her when he would return, she knew that since he had left on Friday, he should have returned for work on Monday. A search party set out on Monday afternoon and found him by the lake later that night. Harold knew that God had answered his prayers and provided both the water and the rescue.

Miracles happen every day. Expect yours!

Lord, help us to keep hope alive when life seems hopeless. Amen.

The Miracle of Heroism

ON JANUARY 13, 1984, as Lennie Scott was crossing the bridge just outside of Washington National Airport, an airplane crashed into the icy water. There were five survivors. One of them, a young woman, let go of her life preserver and started to drown. Several bystanders watched as the young woman sank deeper and deeper into the icy water. Perhaps some of them could not swim, so they did not even consider trying to rescue her. Others may have had on their best clothes and did not want to ruin them. Others probably just waited for someone else to act.

Well, Lennie was that someone. Without regard for his own safety, he jumped in and saved the drowning woman. He managed to hold her up until the helicopters could draw her from the water. Once she was safely rescued, along with the other four survivors, Lennie was rescued.

What compelled Lennie to risk his own life to save someone he did not even know? The young woman and her family believe that Lennie's heroic act was a miracle. It certainly saved their loved one. Was the miracle that she survived the crash or that she survived the water or that she was rescued? Or was the miracle that Lennie was loving enough, unselfish enough, and brave enough to be a hero? Would we have been brave enough to participate in that miracle?

Miracles happen every day. Expect yours!

Lord, give us miracle-expecting and miracle-producing power! Amen.

Miraculous Escapes

The Miracle of the Phone Call

FTER ATTENDING A CONFERENCE in Chicago, Bill Goodwin was on his way to a meeting in West Virginia. He was in the Chicago Airport preparing to board USAir Flight 427 to Pittsburgh. From there he would drive to West Virginia. Bill was looking forward to driving through his hometown in West Virginia. As he made his way to his departure gate, he heard his name. He paused to listen, and sure enough, he was being paged. He checked at the ticket counter and was told to call his assistant immediately.

Bill could not imagine what she wanted. He had just finished a twenty-minute conversation with her. He thought that perhaps she had requested this page before their conversation, and she did not really need to talk with him again. He started to ignore the page, but something told him to check, just to be sure. His assistant was greatly relieved when she heard his voice because she wanted to tell him that his meeting in West Virginia had been canceled. He could take the next flight home. Although he was glad to be going home, he thought it strange that the meeting was canceled. He would later discover that it was the first meeting that had been canceled in eleven years.

After taking the next flight to Atlanta, Bill called his wife while driving to his home in Vinings, Georgia. She was so excited when she heard his voice. She seemed grateful and yet shaken. He asked her what was wrong. She told him that Flight 427, the flight that he almost had boarded, had crashed, leaving no survivors. Bill could not believe what she had said. Why had he been spared? Why had one hundred and thirty-two others died?

Bill has no answers. He just says that he is convinced that the phone call was a miracle sent by God to save him for some special work. When he sings "A charge to keep I have, a God to glorify," it has new meaning.

Miracles happen every day. Expect yours!

Lord, we do not know why some die while others are spared. We just know that we must not waste one minute as we work to glorify You. Amen.

The Missed Tennis Miracle

MARILYN HAD ALWAYS DREAMED of becoming a professional tennis player. She found a tennis racket somewhere, but she had nowhere to practice and no friends to play with. But she was determined, and she decided to practice by herself. She found a place to play in an alley behind a bank. There was a tall brick wall, and she could hit the ball and return it to the wall as hard and as long as she wanted to. That became her private place to work toward her tennis dream, and she went there to practice every day, even on weekends.

One day as she started toward her practice place, something told her not to go. She is not sure whether she had a feeling or heard a voice; all she knows is that she could not go, even though she had never missed a practice. Later she discovered that at the time she had started out to practice, which was her usual time, there was a robbery at the bank. The robber had run out of the bank, across her imaginary tennis court, and into the alley. He was chased by the police, and gun shots were exchanged. Marilyn definitely would have been in the line of fire.

As Marilyn reflects on that day, she knows that God was warning her in a miracluous way. That feeling or voice that kept her at home, even though she had never missed going, was God's way of protecting her. She believes God was saving her for a greater work to be accomplished in the future. It was her miracle missed tennis practice.

Miracles happen every day. Expect yours!

Lord, thank You for saving us from harm. You have many special ways of speaking to us and changing our actions. Amen.

The Miracle of the Chair

GWEN IS A SOCIAL SECURITY EMPLOYEE who was transferred from Atlanta to Dallas in 1990. At the time of her transfer, she asked permission to take her desk chair with her. Gwen had grown attached to her chair and felt that her transfer would be less traumatic with some familiar objects in her new work environment. The chair was an outdated, high-backed executive chair that should have been surplused several years ago. She was told that she could have the chair, but the government would not pay to have it shipped to Dallas. Gwen took the chair home and had it shipped with her household goods.

In 1994, Gwen was transferred to Oklahoma City. Again she took her familiar old chair. She was seated in that chair on the day of the bombing of the federal building in Oklahoma City in 1995. She had just turned around to face her computer when the bomb hit. The blast caused a concrete beam to fall, knocking her from her chair. The chair turned over on top of her, protecting her from the concrete beam and from serious injuries.

Gwen walked away from that deadly bombing with minor injuries. The chair she had carried from Atlanta to Dallas to Oklahoma City had been her miraculous protector. Now she calls that outdated chair her "miracle chair."

Miracles happen every day. Expect yours!

Lord, thank You for those special feelings we develop about certain objects that surround us. They may be Your tools for effecting miracles. Amen.

The Miracle of the Second Chance

LORI EXPERIENCED HER FIRST "second chance" miracle when she was a freshman in college. While driving back to school one day, she lost consciousness and ran off the road. Her car was totally destroyed. It is hard to believe that anyone could have survived, but she did. Lori knew that God had worked a miracle to give her a second chance at life.

Then as a sophomore, Lori was stopped by two men who were asking for directions on her college campus. Although she was in a well-lighted area, the men were able to abduct her at gun point. Lori was frightened and wondered why God had bothered to save her only to have her murdered by two men. It seems that the men were looking for cocaine money, and, finding none, they decided to amuse themselves with Lori. Both men raped her three or four times; then they tried to make her lose her sense of direction by having her lie down on the backseat while they made several turns. Lori tried to remain alert, remembering every right and left turn. While she lay there, Lori prayed that it would not hurt when they killed her and that her family would find her so they would know what had happened to her. She did not want them to worry and wonder whether she was alive.

One of the men promised not to kill her, but she did not believe him. He took his partner home but continued to drive her around in the backseat of the car. Then he stopped the car on a dirt road in front of a bridge. Holding the gun on her, he told her to get out and start to walk across the bridge. Being in shock from her ordeal, Lori lost her balance and fell into a ditch. She tried to hide from her assailant, hoping he could not see her well enough to shoot her. But he found her and told her to get back in the car. This time he let her sit in the front seat next to him, and he released her not far from the campus.

Lori had her second chance miracle. She was alive—battered but not broken. God had saved her.

The men were caught while attempting to rob a convenience store. They had stabbed the clerk twelve times, but the clerk survived. She, too, had her second chance miracle.

Both young women experienced miracles. God gave them a second chance at life. I hope they will live those lives for Him.

Miracles happen every day. Expect yours!

Lord, thank You for the many second chances we have to serve You. Please keep us from wasting these opportunities. Amen.

❧

The Miracle of the Missed Blast

JOYCE LAWYER'S HUSBAND asked her to stop by the bakery to pick up some bread and sweets for a meeting he was hosting. Joyce was happy to make the stop, for she loved the bakery smells. Once inside the bakery, Joyce started looking around at all the delicious things.

Joyce's eyes settled on some delicious looking ginger cookies. They were beautifully big and round, and they reminded Joyce of the ones her grandmother used to make. She stood there for a while, wondering whether she should buy some of them. She kept thinking about her grandmother, and she almost convinced herself not to buy the cookies because she thought they probably would be dry and not nearly as good as her grandmother's.

It was at that moment that Joyce heard a very loud, clear voice. It told her to get out of the bakery right away. The voice was so compelling that Joyce did not hesitate. She moved with haste and exited the store.

As soon as she was safely out of the store and across the street, the store blew up. A gas line had been broken, and the resulting explosion destroyed the bakery. Joyce says that it was a miracle that she heard that voice and was obedient to it.

Miracles happen every day. Expect yours!

Lord, keep us in constant communication with You so that we are listening when You speak to us and provide us with miracles of escape. Amen.

The Miracle of Absence

SOMETHING TOLD MARY ANN not to go to work that day. She operated her own business of dispensing nutrition facts to welfare mothers, and she phoned her office to report her decision to stay at home. Her co-worker affirmed her decision by telling her that everything was under control and that the office had been rather quiet all day.

But the office did not stay quiet for long. Not knowing what kind of assistance the office offered, a distressed mother, high on heroin, entered the office and demanded money. When none was given, she pulled out a gun and started shooting.

That little voice, that something that told Mary Ann not to go to work that day, must have been her guardian angel, for shots went through her chair and all around her desk. It is very likely that she would have been killed had she been sitting there. But she was not there. She was absent. It was a miracle, a miracle of absence. She thanked God that she had listened to that little voice.

Miracles happen every day. Expect yours!

Lord, I covenant with You to listen to that little voice that may speak to me today. Amen.

The Miracle of a Jammed Gun

NEW YORK CITY POLICE DETECTIVE Arlene Beckles was in the beauty shop under the hair dryer when three armed robbers burst in. She noticed that customers were being crowded together in one corner of the shop by one of the robbers, who was shoving a revolver in their faces. A second robber with a semiautomatic was watching every move they made, and a third robber guarded the door.

Arlene managed to move out from under the dryer and hide behind one of the hairdressing stations. She removed her service revolver and hid it under her armpit. She knew that she had only five rounds of ammunition, so she would have to wait for just the right moment. The robbers were busy rifling through purses and taking jewelry; then, when one customer resisted turning over her purse and valuables, a robber noticed Arlene crouched on the floor. He directed his gun at her head. Believing that she had little chance of survival, Arlene decided to draw her gun, announce her police status, and take her chances at saving some of the others. She managed to shoot first one and then the other two robbers, incapacitating two of the three.

Knowing that all five rounds had been fired, there was nothing Arlene could do but pray when the third robber attacked her. She felt the barrel of the gun on her head and heard the trigger being squeezed again and again. But nothing happened. Miraculously, the gun would not fire. It was later determined that some of the bullets in the gun were the wrong size, and the weapon had jammed. Although Arlene accepts the logical reason for the misfire, she knows it was a miracle.

Help arrived, all robbers were apprehended, and Arlene was named Police Officer of the Year. Arlene's survival and ability to keep all customers from harm was truly a miracle.

Miracles happen every day. Expect yours!

Lord, be with our law enforcement officers as they seek to protect us from danger. Amen.

The Miracle of Avoidance

IT WAS ONE OF THOSE NIGHTS when Tami had to work very late. She was tired and sleepy. She began to wonder how she would ever make it all the way home. Like many of us, she had driven the streets so many times that it seemed the car was driving itself. The fact that she failed to concentrate on her driving probably contributed to her sleepiness. Eventually she lost the battle and fell asleep at the wheel.

It is hard to judge how long Tami slept. It probably was only a few seconds, but at thirty-five to forty miles an hour, the car moved quite a distance. Even though cars keep moving, they do not steer themselves. Or do they? As Tami remembers the incident, she wonders.

Tami knows that she had fallen asleep, for she woke up with a start. Her car was headed directly toward a large, brick mailbox and a water hydrant. She did not believe she could avoid a collision, but something happened. The sky above her seemed to light up in an amazingly deep blue color, and the car turned away from the mailbox and water hydrant without her ever touching the wheel. It was a miracle of avoidance. She had been sleeping, but God was awake. He sent His angel to direct that car away from danger.

How many times do we fall asleep on the job and fail to do what we ought to do? How often does our failure result in disaster? But then, there are many times that God takes over and redirects our paths, helping us to avoid danger. Do we remember to thank Him and give Him praise?

Miracles happen every day. Expect yours!

Lord, thank You for waking us up and reminding us of Your constant presence. Amen.

The Miracle of Safety

JULY 1994, WAS THE WETTEST MONTH in the history of Atlanta, Georgia. There were numerous accidents, for the streets were wet and drivers, being impatient, failed to reduce their speed. Sometimes when fast-moving cars hit wet spots, they hydroplane or skim over the water like a speedboat. Such was JoAnn's experience.

JoAnn was driving along a busy highway when she hit a puddle of water. Her car hydroplaned and was completely out of control. She does not know how many other cars she hit or how she finally came to a stop, but she did. And when she did, she was no longer in the driver's seat but in the backseat of her car. Several bystanders rushed to her aid, calling for an ambulance and trying to get her out of her car, which was totally demolished. When they finally pried her door open, they were astonished to see how untouched the interior appeared. Though the outside of the car was gone, the inside was safe and secure.

One of those who had helped to open the car door looked at JoAnn and asked, "Where's the driver?"

JoAnn responded, "I am the driver. I don't know how I got back here."

They tried to get her to go to the hospital, insisting that she had to be hurt. They even explained that one of her car tires was a block away. But JoAnn insisted that she was fine. She felt totally safe. She knew that she had experienced a miracle, a miracle of safety.

Miracles happen every day. Expect yours!

Lord, thank You for keeping us safe in the midst of danger. Help us to be obedient to speed limits and mindful of dangerous conditions so that we can and will assist You in keeping others safe. Amen.

The Miracle of the Fire Wall

PERIODICALLY LOLA HAD HAD ELECTRICAL problems with her car. She wondered if it would ever be repaired properly. Like so many of us, she did not want to admit that she had bought a "lemon." Surely it would not cause her any more problems, she told herself.

Lola drove her car to work and parked in the company lot. As she sat in the car, collecting her belongings, she noticed that the car seemed to be getting hot. Then she saw smoke coming out from under the hood. Her first thought was that the electrical problem had again reared its ugly head. She had just gotten the car from the shop. What was wrong now?

While she sat there, worrying about the car, the smoke became more intense and then flames appeared. Lola came to herself and realized that she had better get out of the car before it exploded. By the time she emerged from the car, there were flames surrounding the hood. But, strangely, the flames seemed to be confined.

Lola stopped two co-workers and asked if they had a car phone and could call 911 to report the fire. Although at first they continued with their seemingly intense conversation, they finally realized that there indeed was an emergency and responded.

Once the fire was extinguished, Lola noticed that the front half of her car was practically melted. When she asked why the fire had not consumed the whole car and caused an explosion, she was told that the car had been built with a fire wall designed to contain the flames.

Lola knew that the fire wall had been her miracle. She remembered how she had stayed in the car once she had reached her destination, and she felt blessed that the fire had not occurred while she was driving. The fire wall had been her protector. She was grateful.

Miracles happen every day. Expect yours!

Lord, thank You for careful engineers who assist You in protecting us every day of our lives. Amen.

The Miracle of the Hump

TIFFANY'S GRANDFATHER SUFFERED from curvature of the spine. The family always felt sad when they looked at Granddad and saw that ugly hump in his back. He was getting shorter and shorter, having already lost five inches of his height. His head seemed to be disappearing into his back, causing him to slump over badly when walking, sitting, or driving. But Granddad was ninety years old, and Tiffany's family was just glad that he was alive.

One day Granddad was in a very bad car accident. He was trying to make a turn in his Lincoln Towncar when he lost control. His car slid across the intersection under an eighteen-wheeler. The impact was so great that the top half of the car was taken off.

Upon arrival, the police and ambulance attendants assumed that they would be removing a headless body from the wreckage. But Granddad had passed out, and because of the hump in his back, his head was so receded that he had slid completely under the truck. Granddad did not have a scratch on his body. Without the hump, he would have been decapitated. All of the attendants were amazed. They proclaimed his survival to be a miracle.

Tiffany is thrilled that her ninety-year-old grandfather has more life to live, thanks to God. In his remaining years, Tiffany will continuously thank God for that miraculous hump!

Miracles happen every day. Expect yours!

Lord, thank You for the infirmities that daily save our lives. Amen.

The Miracle of Resilience

THERE IS SOMETHING SO RESILIENT about youth. Young people can be near death one minute and blessed with good health the next. Consider Mona, a freshman college student who was riding with her friend to Virginia from Atlanta, Georgia. They had participated in a college weekend that was designed to let them have some fun before final examinations. The two were late in leaving because they had planned to stay in Atlanta until the last party was over.

Just before Mona fell asleep in the car, she noticed that her friend was driving one hundred and twenty miles per hour. She started to say something, but she was just too sleepy. Suddenly, she woke up with a start and whispered a prayer, for she knew they were about to have an accident. Her friend had lost control of the car, and they were headed over the edge of a cliff.

According to two off-duty ambulance drivers who observed the accident, the car seemed to climb up a mountain, hit some trees, roll over, and burst into flames. Just before hitting the trees, both Mona and her friend were thrown from the car. Neither was wearing a seat belt, but, in this case, that may have been a blessing. Mona's friend escaped without a scratch, but Mona was knocked unconscious. Her friend tried mouth-to-mouth resuscitation, and then the two off-duty ambulance drivers reached them and started to administer first aid.

Mona suffered a broken collar bone, a fractured spine, and multiple lacerations. It was feared that she would not be able to walk again. Mona knew her situation was serious, but all she could do was pray for forgiveness. She knew that she should not have been in a car that was being driven at such a high speed, and she knew that she should have done something about it. She prayed that God would give her a second chance to make something positive out of the wild party-going life she had been living.

With God's help, and with her youthful resilience, Mona made a complete recovery. She is a changed person—a serious college student and a committed Christian. She knows that her survival was a miracle. Her rapid recovery witnesses to her youthful resilience. That, too, is a miracle!

Miracles happen every day. Expect yours!

Lord, forgive us for being disobedient to the laws that are enacted to protect us. Amen.

The Miracle of the Seat Belt

SHARON WAS HEADED HOME on the expressway after attending a birthday party. It had been raining all day and most of the night. There were puddles of water all along the expressway. Sharon hit one of those puddles and lost control of her car. After skidding off the highway on two wheels and turning over several times, she landed in a twenty-foot ditch surrounded by construction. The seat belt, which probably had saved her life, had cut her throat, and a bone was sticking out of her left leg. Still, Sharon managed to get out of the car and cry for help. No one heard her. The construction had hidden her from view.

After crying for help for about an hour, Sharon, convinced that she would die in that ditch, decided to try to crawl up the embankment to the road. She began to pray. She knew that she was bleeding at the throat and that her leg was broken near the ankle, but she had to crawl out of that ditch. She grabbed bits of shrubbery and started to pull herself up. She would climb up two feet and slide back down three feet. She was covered with mud and blood, but she kept praying and climbing. Exhausted, she finally made it to the road. She lay by the side of the road in the rain, hoping that someone would see her.

Dozens of cars passed, but no one stopped to help. Sharon cried and cried for help. Finally, two young men stopped. They asked what had happened, noticed her car in the ditch, and left. Sharon was devastated. She knew that she had been left to die, but she realized how frightening she must look covered with blood, mud, and rain. Shortly afterward, the police came, called an ambulance, and took Sharon to the hospital. She can only assume that the young men called the police. All she knows for sure is that when her car was recovered, it had been stripped, and her purse and other belongings had been stolen. She wonders whether the young men helped her, returned to rob her, or both.

Sharon remained conscious in the emergency room and heard the diagnosis. She had a broken ankle, crushed ribs, slight concussion, and a deep gash on the throat and shoulder from the seat belt. The doctors said that her survival was a miracle, and that the seat belt had played a major role in saving her life.

Sharon spent three months in the hospital. Her ankle had to be reconstructed. Muscle tissue from her shoulder and skin from her thigh were used to make a new ankle. The miracle that began when the seat belt saved her life continued when the doctor constructed a new ankle from parts of the body that God had made for her.

Sharon left the hospital on crutches, moved to a walker, and then to a cane. Now she walks on her own with a slight limp. Sharon is thankful for the miracles that have been a part of her recovery. She feels that God has spared her for the specific purpose of being the best mother her daughter could have. She has accepted that challenge.

Miracles happen every day. Expect yours!

Lord, make us aware of the miracles in our lives. Help us to realize that every miracle of survival challenges us to fulfill the purpose for which we were born. Amen.

The Miracle of Air Bags and Vests

OFFICER OWEN DUNCAN WAS AT WORK in his police cruiser in the hours just before dawn when his miracle occurred. He did not know that a drunken woman was speeding toward him. He did not know that she was driving the wrong way on the interstate highway that was a part of his patrol. He did not know that another police car had already flashed signals, which she had ignored. He did not know that she had raced through a toll booth and that she was seconds away from him.

When he saw her headlights, he tried to warn her by flashing his lights in her direction. Before he had time to react, she was crashing through his windshield. Then his miracle occurred. His air bags inflated upon impact, and his bulletproof vest protected his chest. He was able to get out of his car without injury and proceed to pull the drunken woman from her car, which had burst into flames. She suffered multiple injuries, but she probably would have died without the officer's assistance.

Officer Duncan says that he did not have time to contemplate the end of his life. He just knew that he was spared and the driver of the other vehicle needed his help. He reflected on the miraculous invention of air bags that go unseen until needed. He was thankful for his bulletproof vest, which had not protected him from the anticipated bullet but from the unanticipated collision. These events were miraculous, and his escaping without injury was a miracle all its own.

Miracles happen every day. Expect yours!

Lord, thank You for the safety devices that work with You to save our lives. Amen.

The Miracle of Road Safety

THE BRYSON FAMILY WAS HEADED toward Grandma's to celebrate Christmas. Their car was loaded with gifts and children and all the many other things normally packed for long trips. Prior to leaving, they did what they always do. They prayed for God's traveling mercies. They wanted to arrive safely, without being injured or injuring anyone. They started out with confidence that God would grant that request.

Once they entered the highway, they set the car on cruise control and relaxed for what would be an eight-hour ride. Before they knew it, they had hit a large amount of debris in the road. There was a good deal of noise, but there appeared to be no damage to either the car or its passengers. They continued on their way until it was time to stop for gas. As soon as they were safely off the highway and at the gas station, the car seemed to sink. When they got out of the car, both front tires were flat. How could they have traveled so far from the collision with the debris on two front tires? Then they remembered their prayer for traveling mercies.

But their mercies—and what they later recognized as miracles—did not stop there: Although they did not have two spare tires, there was a tow truck at the gas station; and a repair shop just happened to be open; and the tires miraculously had remained inflated until they were at the gas station, safely off the highway; and they had not had an accident even though they had been traveling at cruise control speed. Yes, they had experienced a miracle of road safety.

Miracles happen every day. Expect yours!

Lord, remind us to invoke Your blessings as we travel each day. You so often grant us traveling mercies even though we fail to ask or thank You. Amen.

The Potato Chip Miracle

SUSAN AND ONE OF HER GIRLFRIENDS had journeyed by car from New Orleans to Baton Rouge. While in Baton Rouge, they had visited Southern University. Now they were quite content as they began their return trip home. They ate, purchased gas, and headed for the highway. Just as they approached the entrance ramp, Susan had a craving for "Salt-N-Vinegar" potato chips. After stopping to purchase some, she drove onto the highway.

Although Susan thought that she could drive all the way home, she found herself tiring and asked her friend to complete the journey. Once the girls had exchanged places, Susan began to relax and enjoy her potato chips. Then something very strange happened. The bag of chips seemed to jump out of her hands and roll completely under the dashboard. Susan was sure that she had had a good grip on the bag, and she could not explain the strange sensation of the bag literally jumping out of her hands. But because she yearned for another chip, she quickly went under the dashboard, chasing the dancing bag.

Before her friend, who was driving, knew what had happened, a car ran a yield sign and smashed into Susan's car on the passenger side, where seconds earlier she had been sitting. The impact threw Susan's slim, ninety-two pound, five-feet two-inch body completely under the dashboard, knocking her unconscious. The car spun several times and landed in a ditch.

Susan regained consciousness to discover her friend knocked out by the air bag but otherwise all right. LaShon also was spared serious injury. The passenger side where she had been sitting had no air bag, and, in all likelihood, she would have crashed into the windshield if she had not followed the potato chip bag under the dashboard.

Susan lost her car, but not her life—all because of a craving for "Salt-N-Vinegar" potato chips that miraculously danced out of her hands.

Miracles happen every day. Expect yours!

Lord, thank You for watching over us as we travel. Teach us to drive with care and to make good use of the safety devices provided within our vehicles. Amen.

The Miracle of the Tires

NICOLE WAS PRAYING EACH INCH of the way as she traveled the icy road home. It was a dark and foggy Illinois night, and she knew that danger was possible at every turn. But Nicole felt that she was a good driver who was accustomed to the wintry conditions. Believing that the cars ahead of her were moving at the same pace that she was, Nicole was startled when she suddenly found herself about to hit a stalled car. To avoid a collision, she slammed on her brakes and, hitting a sheet of ice, skidded off the road into the woods.

As her car slid through the woods, Nicole feared the worst. She prayed for a miracle. How could she escape the trees that surrounded her? Then she came to a sudden stop. She was alert, awake, and unhurt. What had happened?

Nicole got out of her car and saw that the tree she had hit was encircled by rows of tires. The tires had cushioned the impact and had protected her from injury. She had not escaped the trees, but God had miraculously provided tires of protection.

Miracles happen every day. Expect yours!

Lord, thank You for providing protection in the most miraculous ways. Amen.

Miraculous Births

The Miracle of Movement

FTER HAVING EXPERIENCED several months of problems in her pregnancy, Frances was told that the fetus was dead. She had heard what her doctor had said, but she just could not accept the truth of his statement. How could her baby be dead? Surely he was mistaken. She refused in her heart to believe that her months of suffering would not yield a healthy, live child.

Frances started doing the only thing she knew to do. She started having daily and nightly conversations with God. She kept talking to God, asking Him to let her child live. She knew that if the child was dead, it would soon abort. But she knew God was able, and she prayed that her child would wake up from its deathlike stillness.

Acting on faith, she decided to spend her summer teaching summer school. She felt that her child would survive and that she should not be idle waiting for disaster. While standing at the chalkboard one day, explaining an assignment, she felt a thump in her stomach. Had the supposedly dead fetus actually moved? Silently, she began to pray, "Lord, I am Yours, and the child within is Yours. Let Your will be done."

After school was dismissed, Frances drove to the doctor's office, praying all the way. The doctor examined her. He pressed, poked, listened, and looked puzzled. Then he took her hand and said, "It's going to be all right. The baby is moving, and all signs look good."

Frances left the office thanking and praising God. The words of Mark 11:24—"So I tell you, whatever you ask for in prayer, believe that you have received it, and it will be yours"—stayed on her lips and in her heart.

Today she has a lovely twenty-three-year-old daughter.

Miracles happen every day. Expect yours!

Lord, help us to believe in Your movement-giving power. Even dead bones can live. Amen.

The Miracle of Breathing

WAYNE AND CATHY HAD ALWAYS WANTED a baby, and when they were finally expecting one, they were thrilled. They dreamed of having a fine, bright, and beautiful baby. They did not care whether it was a girl or a boy; they just wanted a healthy baby.

When the baby arrived, they noticed the doctor's guarded expression. Something was wrong; the baby was not breathing. The doctors hooked him up to a breathing machine. Their beautiful little boy had tubes sticking out of everywhere. He could not survive without the machine.

Immediately Cathy started to pray. She begged God to let her baby live. Being a strong and healthy athlete, Wayne did not understand how his son could not breathe. His son had to be strong; his son could not possibly need machines and tubes. But little Nicholas was not strong. He did need life support.

The parents asked, "How long can we keep our baby on this breathing machine?" The doctors advised them to give Nicholas a week. If he did not start to breathe on his own by the end of the week, he probably would not survive. That gave Cathy a week to wait and pray. She entered into fervent prayer. She led her husband in prayer; she led her family in prayer. She decided to be constant in prayer. Her baby would start to breathe on his own. She would see to it!

By the end of the week, Nicholas still was not breathing on his own, and the doctors advised that the machine be disconnected. Reluctantly, Wayne and Cathy agreed. The machine was unplugged, and the tubes were removed. As soon as this was done, Nicholas started to breathe. He was breathing on his own. It was a miracle!

Miracles happen every day. Expect yours!

Lord, thank You for everyday miracles. Every breath we take is a miracle. Amen.

The Miracle of Recovery

RYAN WAS BORN EIGHT WEEKS PREMATURE. He suffered kidney damage, blood loss, a bowel obstruction, and possible brain damage. Noting this damage to his vital organs, the doctors described his condition as "universally fatal" and disconnected him from a kidney dialysis machine.

It appeared that little Ryan would surely die. The doctors had predicted it. But his parents would not submit to what seemed to be the inevitable. They believed it was wrong not to give Ryan every chance of survival. So they went to court to force continuation of the dialysis and to find another hospital that would treat their son.

Within weeks they had found a hospital in another state that agreed to treat Ryan. In a few short months, Ryan was released from that hospital with his family. He had defied the earlier grim predictions. He had experienced a miraculous recovery. He was going home.

Ryan's family said that the only way they could explain Ryan's recovery was that it had to have been a miracle. They had worked to save Ryan by going to court to order the continuation of treatment, and they had believed that their son would live. But the recovery that allowed a smiling baby to leave the hospital in the arms of his parents can only be explained as a miracle.

Miracles happen every day. Expect yours!

Lord, give us faith when even the doctors have none. All things are possible for those who believe. Amen.

A Miracle of Disobedience

HIS NAME IS WALTER LITTLE, and he is supposed to be dead. But his grandparents disobeyed the doctors, and his predicted life span of six months to one year has long since been surpassed.

He was born with hydrocephalus, a disorder usually characterized by an abnormal amount of cerebrospinal fluid, enlargement of the skull, and wasting away of the brain. The doctors told his grandparents not to move or touch him unless absolutely necessary, but they disobeyed.

Walter feels that the loving touch and prayers of his grandparents gave him life that has lasted into adulthood. He says, "I am a miracle. If it wasn't for God and my grandparents, I wouldn't be here."

Walter lives a full adult life as a city employee. He also has been a volunteer fireman for ten years, and this work has provided opportunities for him to provide assistance in times of disaster. He says that even as a child he was fascinated with fire fighting equipment and the relief they could bring to victims.

Writing, however, is Walter's favorite thing. This is especially miraculous because of the wasting away of the brain usually caused by his condition. He coordinates a local newsletter, edits a newsletter for his computer club, and serves as the club's historian. He also uses his writing skills on his job as a part of the city's administrative staff.

Walter also volunteers at children's hospitals, telling patients with similar disabilities about his miracle. He says, "Don't let anyone tell you that you can't do something. You are only limited by your mind."

Miracles happen every day. Expect yours!

Lord, give comfort, help, and strength to those living with medical disorders. Thank You for the victories that come through love and prayer. Amen.

The Miracle of Safe Arrival

TERRI WAS EXPECTING A BABY. She carefully had planned for a trip to the hospital and the skillful delivery team that would assist her. But things did not go as planned. Terri went into labor at home. She thought she would have time to get to the hospital, but the pains started coming so fast that she had to call an ambulance. She also called her friend Wendy and her husband, Paul.

Both her friend and her husband arrived before the ambulance. When Wendy saw that the baby was coming, she called 911, asking for instructions on how to deliver a baby. She carefully relayed the instructions to Paul, who delivered his son.

Not only did Wendy relay instructions, but she also prayed that Paul's hands would be sure and deliberate as they grabbed the tiny newborn. Her prayers became more intense when she noticed that the baby was not breathing. Again, she asked 911 for directions and passed those on to Paul.

Through all of this, Wendy never stopped praying. She knew that none of them was experienced in childbirth and they needed a miracle for the safe arrival of this child. Paul carefully did as instructed and resuscitated his son. When they finally heard a cry, they knew that they had participated in one of God's special miralces. It was the miracle of safe arrival.

Today that safe arrival is a happy, healthy child, and Terri, Paul, and Wendy are extremely grateful.

Miracles happen every day. Expect yours!

Lord, thank You for dedicated 911 workers, and thank You for faithful friends who are constant in prayer. Most of all, thank You for the safe arrival of newborns, who have the opportunity to live for You. Amen.

The Miracle of Neonatal Care

HOW EARLY IS TOO EARLY for a premature birth? Is five weeks too early? Seven weeks? Ten weeks? How about thirteen weeks? When one survives being more than three months premature, I call it a miracle.

Melody knew that it was too early to go into labor, yet she was sure that the baby was coming. She was glad that the hospital had an outstanding neonatal unit and that her child would receive excellent care in what was called the preemie nursery, but she was scared. She felt that it would take a miracle for her child to survive.

Tiny Alyssa was born thirteen weeks premature. She weighed only one pound and fourteen ounces. She was so small that she easily fit in the palm of one hand. Was her heart developed? How about her lungs? How could internal organs be that small and still function? Melody was told that Alyssa's chances of survival were slim. Melody started praying for her miracle.

Alyssa had to stay in the hospital neonatal unit for sixty-one days. During that time the committed doctors and nurses helped her to breathe, eat, and survive. Melody spent those days praying for and loving her daughter. It was a combination of the medical care and the love and prayers that worked to effect the miracle. Alyssa emerged from the hospital a healthy, happy baby.

Miracles happen every day. Expect yours!

Lord, thank You for the medical technology that You have given us. Keep us ever mindful that even our access to that technology is a miracle from You. Amen.

The Miracle Baby

VICKEY WAS FIVE MONTHS PREGNANT. She and her husband, Lawrence, planned a wonderful cruise as their last vacation together before the expected birth. The doctors told Vickey that everything was fine and that she should have no difficulty on the cruise.

The couple was to start the trip from Orlando, and they checked in a little early. Vickey did not feel well, but not wanting to alarm her husband, she said nothing. Believing that a walk would settle her stomach, she asked Lawrence to walk with her to a nearby shopping mall as there was plenty of time before departure. But her discomfort increased, and when she saw a few drops of blood in her urine, she decided to tell Lawrence. They rushed back to the ship's infirmary, but the staff there knew they were ill equipped to handle the problem.

Vickey and Lawrence were taken to the Arnold Palmer Hospital in Orlando, which has a fully equipped neonatal unit. Vickey was in labor, but in light of the length of her gestation, every effort was made to stop the labor from proceeding any further.

From the moment they entered the hospital, Vickey was impressed with the staff. They told her that they were praying for her and that they believed God would take care of her baby.

The attempts to stop the labor failed. The doctors told Vickey and Lawrence that they could continue with drugs that might stop the labor; however, those drugs might harm either Vickey or the baby or both. They also warned that if the labor continued, a very small underdeveloped baby would be born with little chance of survival. The couple asked for time to be alone to pray and ask for guidance. The medical staff said that they also would be in prayer.

As soon as they were alone, Vickey's baby started kicking vigorously, and Vickey interpreted those kicks to mean that her baby was fighting for survival and that she had to fight too. She told her husband that she wanted to forget the drugs; she and the baby would take their chances.

Little Lawton was born twenty-four hours later. He weighed just one pound and ten ounces. He was placed in the neonatal unit with other preemies. The prayers for his survival intensified. Babies in the incubators to the right and left of him died, but Lawton kept kicking. He stayed at Arnold Palmer for two months, and then was flown to the hospital where his parents had intended for him to be born.

Today Lawton is a healthy baby. His parents call him their miracle baby, and so he is.

Miracles happen every day. Expect yours!

Lord, teach us to keep fighting to survive against all odds. Even unborn babies know that is what You would have us to do. Amen.

The Miracle of Incompatibility

LIZA WAS THE BABY OF HER FAMILY, and she had always wanted someone else to be younger so that she could have authority over someone. But, as the baby, it seemed that everyone always had authority over her. Then Liza found out that her sister was pregnant. She knew that the doctors had told her sister that she would never be able to have children because of egg and sperm incompatibility. Although Liza was too young to comprehend the full meaning of that statement, she knew it was a miracle that her sister was pregnant, and she was grateful there soon would be someone in the family younger than she was.

Liza anxiously awaited the baby's birth, but it seemed to take forever. After seven months, she was sure that she could not wait for her sister to carry the baby nine months. But when she came home from school one day to learn that her sister was in the hospital, she wished that it was the ninth and not the seventh month. She was afraid for both her sister and the baby. Liza went with her parents to the hospital.

The doctors informed the family that they had done all in their power to prolong the labor, but it was not working. The baby was coming, and there was not much hope for survival. Within hours, Liza was looking at her new niece, who weighed only two pounds and two ounces. The baby's lungs were underdeveloped, and when she cried, her mouth moved but she barely made a sound.

Miraculously, the baby survived and is living proof that God is in control of reproduction, even reproduction thought impossible due to egg and sperm incompatibility.

Miracles happen every day. Expect yours!

Lord, thank You for saving babies who are underweight and underdeveloped. We know that with You all things are possible. Amen.

The Miracle of Being Held

CHASE WAS BORN SIXTEEN WEEKS PREMATURE. He weighed less than two pounds and was given no chance of survival. For almost three hours he clung to life on a ventilator, but the doctors informed his parents that there was no hope. The young parents were devastated. How could they lose the child they had prayed for? What had gone wrong? Why wasn't he strong enough to survive? Why had he been born so early?

Finally, accepting the inevitable, the parents asked that they at least be given the opportunity to hold the baby for the last moments of his life. They knew that somehow they had to cram a lifetime of loving into a few moments of holding and praying.

The doctors disconnected the ventilator and placed young Chase in his parents arms. They held him, loved him, and told him of the wonderful things they had planned for his future. Even as the doctors observed this touching scene, they prepared the death certificate. But the parents kept loving, holding, and praying. Then the miracle happened. Chase gasped for air and revived.

Miracles happen every day. Expect yours!

Lord, thank You for never giving up on us, even when we give up on ourselves. Your miracles happen even while we dare to hold and love. Amen.

The Miracle Heart Transplant

JUST FOUR DAYS AFTER BIRTH, baby Eddie underwent a heart transplant. At the time, he was the youngest person ever to successfully undergo such an operation. And ten years later, Eddie is alive and well. It is a miracle of a heart transplant!

Eddie's survival as a normal healthy child is a source of inspiration to many families with sick babies. A new heart, if available, can be transplanted, and healthy survival is possible. Miracles do happen.

Eddie was born with an underdevelopment of the left side of the heart. This condition is usually fatal shortly after birth. Some children die within days, while others live a few weeks. As a part of the miracle God had planned, Eddie was born at Loma Linda University Children's Hospital, where experiments were being conducted on infant heart transplants. A baboon heart had been transplanted into a human infant just one year before Eddie's birth. Eddie's mother was willing to try another such transplant even though the first infant had survived less than a month. She was desperate.

Three days after his birth, a human heart was available. Although the doctors were not sure how long Eddie would survive, his mother prayed for one day at a time. She knew that each day she had with her son would be precious. God answered her prayers, and her son is now expected to live to adulthood and have a normal lifespan. It was indeed a miracle heart transplant.

Miracles happen every day. Expect yours!

Lord, thank You for innovative doctors who are willing to use their talents to effect miraculous feats. We know that all they accomplish comes from You. Amen.

The One-Pound Six-Ounce Miracle

IN THE SIXTH MONTH OF HER PREGNANCY, LaVerne, who was suffering from extremely high blood pressure, was rushed to the hospital. She was diagnosed as having toxemia, an abnormal condition associated with the presence of toxic substances in the blood. She was so sick that she could neither talk nor even open her eyes. Her family was informed that the baby had to be delivered as soon as possible. The delivery would be risky, and both LaVerne and the baby might not survive. The short duration of the pregnancy did not give the baby much chance of survival, and the toxemia did not give LaVerne much chance.

All the family could do was pray, and they prayed that both mother and child would survive. The family felt that if a little prayer was good, a lot of prayer was better. So they prayed continuously for several hours. Even while the prayers continued, LaVerne delivered a one-pound six-ounce baby girl. Both mother and daughter needed blood transfusions, and the family members gladly donated blood.

Later in the week, LaVerne opened her eyes, began to talk, and was informed of the birth of her daughter. Although LaVerna stayed in the hospital only a week and a half, her little daughter had to stay in the hospital two months—until she had gained five pounds.

Although no one on the hospital staff really gave baby Lisa much chance of survival, her family believed that God was testing their faith. Their prayers had helped them to pass the test. Both mother and daughter had survived.

One year later, the family and hospital staff attended Lisa's first birthday party. Looking at the bright and healthy baby, they marveled at the miracle that had happened in their presence.

Miracles happen every day. Expect yours!

Lord, thank You for miraculous births and praying families. Amen.

Miraculous Faith

The Miracle of Sitting

HER NAME IS ROSA PARKS, and in 1955, by the simple act of sitting, she became the agent of miraculous reform.

She had just gotten off work as a seamstress for Montgomery Fair, a downtown department store in Montgomery, Alabama. She was tired, and she took a seat in the first row behind the section reserved for white people. But the Cleveland Avenue bus became crowded, and the bus driver ordered her and three other black passengers to move back so that white boarding passengers could be seated. But if she obeyed, she would have had to stand. Although the other black passengers complied with the request, she continued to sit, and she was arrested.

By sitting, Rosa Parks sparked a bus boycott that lasted three hundred and eighty-one days and resulted in the desegregation of Montgomery buses. The leader of that boycott was an unknown Montgomery pastor who emerged as the most powerful civil rights leader in the nation. His name was Martin Luther King, Jr.

What if Rosa Parks had moved back quietly with the other three passengers? Would the civil rights movement have had to wait for another miracle? Probably. But Rosa Parks was used by God to effect a miracle, a miracle of sitting. Because she refused to give up her seat, the nation was never the same. Thank God for Rosa Parks!

Miracles happen every day. Expect yours!

Lord, thank You for the mother of the civil rights movement and for all who dare to effect change when they encounter injustice. Amen.

The Miracle of Survival

ON MARCH 27, 1994, a tornado ripped through Piedmont, Alabama, killing twenty people and injuring ninety others. One of those injured was Colby Bowman, a four-year-old who spent more that two weeks in a coma after his head was split open by a flying piece of wood. The fact that this child survived at all is a miracle!

Colby had been on an outing with his great-grandparents when the tornado struck. The flying wooden board fractured his skull and left an exposed blood clot over a portion of his brain. He was not expected to survive, but, miraculously, he did. After spending two months in the hospital and undergoing therapy to relearn how to talk, walk, and feed himself, Colby rode a tricycle around the hospital's garden during a party to celebrate his release.

One can only wonder why God spared the life of Colby while twenty others perished. God must have a great work for Colby to do. We can only hope and pray that he will be faithful in carrying out his mission. He was blessed to be a blessing!

Miracles happen every day. Expect yours!

Lord, help us to respond to the messages You reveal to us through survival. Each day we survive we have a mission and purpose to fulfill. Help us to be faithful to it. Amen.

The Miracle of the Door

DOROTHY IS THE SEVENTH of eight children born to a sharecropper and domestic worker in rural Alabama. She grew up in a two-room country shack that her father had built with his own hands. Although her parents were not able to provide much materially, they instilled Christian principles in all of their children.

Dorothy was a dreamer. She wanted more than sharecropping could provide, and she was not a very good field hand. She resented having to miss two months of school at harvesttime. She dreamed of going to college and making something of herself. She heard about a work scholarship program that would allow students like herself to work their way through Tuskegee Institute. She knew that program would be her way out.

While still in high school, Dorothy was hired to take care of an elderly woman in the landowner's "big house." She did not know that she would be asked to sleep on the floor and eat her food on the stove door. The beds and the table were not to be used by "nigras." Dorothy did not understand why she was not being treated like a human being, so she quit. But when she became a senior in high school and desperately needed money for college, she decided to try again to find work.

This time she went to an employment agency and got a job as a domestic. She was overjoyed, for she would actually be making money. As she proudly walked up to the front door of her future employer, she was stopped by a woman who asked, "What do you want?" When she explained that she had been sent by the employment agency, she was told, "Didn't you know to come to the backdoor?" Again, Dorothy almost quit, but she wanted and needed that job. She decided that if she was ever to reach her goal, she had to be obedient and go to the backdoor. Someday she would own her own front door.

The door became the source of Dorothy's miracle. She was transformed from a poor sharecropper's daughter to a college graduate who currently is a consultant for the State of Georgia Department of Technical and Adult Education. She says that she went through the backdoor in order to open the front door. She opened that door, and today she indeed owns her own front door. She has experienced her miracle.

Miracles happen every day. Expect yours!

Lord, help us to remember that no one can drag us so low as to make us hate him or her. Love has redeemed us all. Amen.

The Miracle No-Hitter

JIM ABBOTT, A UNIVERSITY OF MICHIGAN baseball player, won the Sullivan Award as the best amateur athlete. It was the first time the award had been given to a baseball player, and Jim was quite an unusual baseball player. He was a pitcher with an eleven and one record, and he had been born without a right hand.

Can you even imagine trying to play baseball without a right hand? Well, Jim never considered not playing. He said, "No one ever told me that I couldn't do it. I was always encouraged and welcomed." Perhaps those who encouraged and welcomed him helped to make his dream come true.

Jim had always wanted to be a professional baseball player. He had to work twice as hard as anyone else. He had a special glove, and he had real talent. The California Angels took note and drafted him on the first round. Although many wondered whether that was a wise decision, all doubts were put to rest when, in his first season in 1989, he pitched a no-hitter. It was a miracle.

Miracles happen every day. Expect yours!

Lord, help us to encourage and enable others to make the best use of their talents. With faith and trust in You, there are no disabilities, only opportunities. Amen.

The Miracle of Crossing the River

IN 1978, A JOURNALIST by the name of John Everingham fell in love with a Laotian woman named Kayo. Laos was under the rule of communism, and John asked several people how to get Kayo out of Laos so that they could marry and start a new life together. John was told that he would have to get her across the river and that would be impossible. In fact, he was told, "You can't get there from here!" John knew that it would take a miracle, but he expected one.

As he surveyed the situation, he decided that the only way to cross the river was in a boat because Kayo could not swim. They would have to dodge rifle bullets and grenades that were constantly being thrown in the water, and he would have to build up his stamina so that he could row the distance required. But John was determined. He started running, quit smoking, and worked out every day. In the process, he broke his collarbone, but he would not give up. He knew that what he wanted for himself and the woman he loved was worth dying for.

After several failures, John and Kayo made it across the river. They married, moved to Australia, and had a son. John knew that he needed a miracle, but he did not sit around and wait for it to happen. He worked to make it happen.

Miracles happen every day. Expect yours!

Lord, we all want miraculous things to happen in our lives, but most of us expect You to do all the work. Where we are able, teach us to assist You. Amen.

The Miracle of Reunion

ELMER JACKSON WAS A POOR MAN. With four young sons to feed, he and his wife could barely make ends meet. Then Mrs. Jackson was diagnosed with cancer, and the medical bills took almost everything they had. Knowing that she would not survive, she asked her husband to promise her that he would keep the boys together.

After his wife's death, Elmer could not believe that anyone could take his sons away. But the Department of Social Services paid him a visit and announced that it would be in the interest of the children to move them to foster homes. Elmer was not able to provide for his boys, but he remembered his promise to his wife and vowed to get them all back together.

The boys were held in different homes because nobody would take them all. One was very badly mistreated; his leg was broken, and because he was believed to be retarded, he was sterilized. The other boys cried themselves to sleep each night because they missed their parents and their brothers. Elmer knew that he had to get them back even if it took a miracle. He started praying for one, and then he started acting.

Elmer set out to find a job that paid well and to build a house with his own hands that would accommodate his family. He knew that he had to buy clothes and maintain a certain appearance before anyone in the welfare office would even consider his case. But Elmer did all of these things. He even found a woman who agreed to become his wife and help him care for his sons when he regained their custody.

It took years, but Elmer accomplished his dream. His miracle of reunion with his sons took place. With God's help, he was able to keep the promise he had made to their mother.

Miracles happen every day. Expect yours!

Lord, thank You for family. Help us to appreciate our families more and to do all in our power to keep our families together. Amen.

The Miracle of $1.50

HER NAME WAS MARY MCLEOD BETHUNE, and she wanted literacy for her newly liberated people. Although she was aware of the need for reading, writing, and arithmetic, she felt that there was an even more urgent need for learning the simple fundamentals of farming, homemaking, and cleanliness. She decided that she should be the one to start just such a school.

With one dollar and fifty cents and her young son, she headed for Daytona Beach, Florida. The deprived conditions that she found there convinced her that it was the ideal place for her school. Her school would focus on practical skills such as farming, cooking, sewing, and health care. She would teach young women to be fine wives and mothers. Those young women would, in turn, raise their children so that they could live successfully in America, which had been opened to them as a freed people.

It would take a miracle for a school to be founded with the meager amount that was left of her savings. But somehow, with only one dollar and fifty cents and five little girls from eight to twelve years old, Mary did it. She served as the founder and principal of the Daytona Educational and Industrial School for Negro girls.

Being blessed with musical talent, Mary trained the girls to sing and entertain at meetings in and around Daytona Beach. There was a millionaire in one of the audiences, and he became a supporter of the school. His name was John D. Rockefeller.

Mrs. Bethune taught her girls to care for themselves and their families. She taught them that they could do anything they really wanted to. She taught them to believe in miracles. They listened to her, and they believed her.

Mrs. Bethune's school for girls eventually merged with Cookman Institute, a men's college, and is now known as Bethune-Cookman College. It all began with a dream and one dollar and fifty cents. It was a miracle!

Miracles happen every day. Expect yours!

Lord, teach us to dream big dreams. We believe that with You all things are possible. Amen.

The Miracle of Vibration

TAMMY SAT AT THE FOOTBALL GAME, watching the high school drill team. She thought, "I can do that too." She would just have to carefully count each step, turn, and kick, coordinating everything with vibrations. Tammy could neither hear the music nor the beat of the drum; she could only feel them. You see, Tammy is deaf.

Even Tammy's sister thought that she could not make the drill team, but Tammy expected a miracle. When she attended the tryouts, she was nervous. But so was everyone else. They made mistakes, and so did she. It appeared that Tammy tried a little harder, coordinated her movements a little better, counted a little more precisely, and concentrated on those miraculous vibrations. She was better than the girls who could hear, and she showed her sister. She made the drill team.

Tammy's sign language interpreter was not surprised at all. Working with Tammy over the past four years, he has learned that she can do anything she sets her mind to. He has seen her master college prep courses, write and deliver speeches, and participate in the Super Honor Roll and Beta Club.

Tammy's classmates have learned to respect her. She says that though they used to ignore her, now they are friendly and helpful. Tammy has gained new confidence and self-esteem through her achievements. She helps her classmates as much as possible, and she even helps her doubting sister with her homework.

Tammy believes in miracles. She plans to go to college and become a business manager or a musician. And she will!

Miracles happen every day. Expect yours!

Lord, thank You for vibrations that allow those who are hearing impaired to participate fully in activities we too often take for granted. Amen.

The Miracle of Special Twins

IN 1970, TWINS, CHRIS AND COREY, were born with muscular dystrophy. It was predicted that they would not live more than two or three years. They would never learn to walk, and they would not even be able to turn over without assistance. But their mother, Jackie, thanked God for her beautiful boys.

Jackie somehow communicated to her sons the sheer pleasure of life, even life in a wheelchair. Chris and Corey were chosen as muscular dystrophy poster children in 1980; they led their high school football team's victory parades from their wheelchairs; and they cheered from the sidelines at the feats that others could accomplish all by themselves. They have never voiced negative feelings of self-pity or wasted precious time—time that was never thought possible for them—feeling sorry for themselves. Chris and Corey just led and cheered any way they could.

These twins who were not expected to live more than two or three years entered college in their electronic wheelchairs. They needed personal care attendants to help them get into and out of bed and to attend to their personal needs, but they graduated with 3.7 grade point averages. At age twenty-five, Chris is an administrator at his college alma mater and Corey is teaching in a high school.

Jackie has learned to live her days one at a time. So often she did not know where she would get the money for the personal care or the three surgeries that the twins had to undergo or the university tuition, but she says that you don't need a ticket to board a train until you are ready to board. She has learned to let go and let God. God has given and provided for her very special, miraculous twins.

Miracles happen every day. Expect yours!

Lord, teach us to meet each day believing that You will provide. We thank You for that blessed assurance. Amen.

The Miracle Church

REV. TEASLEY LOOKS AT THE BUILDING in which he and his nearly two hundred members worship and says, "This is a miracle church." He says this because he remembers when his congregation had fourteen members, no place to worship, and no hymnals. But for the past seven years, the members have spent every spare minute, even vacations, building a beautiful sanctuary and fellowship hall.

When Rev. Teasley first became the pastor, they worshiped in an abandoned nightclub. They eventually saved enough money to buy a lot. Another savings drive produced enough money for the foundation, but then the people felt that they had gone as far as they could go. Rev. Teasley convinced them that God had a miracle church for them, but they would have to be the instruments used to effect the miracle. He challenged each member to raise one hundred dollars and taught them to build—being a homebuilder by trade.

Some of the men climbed scaffolding, raised roof beams, and placed shingles while some of the women led the painting crew. Those who could not build prepared food for those who could. Even friends helped, for when they saw how dedicated the members were, they decided to join them. When the church was completed, it was debt-free because of the free labor. Faith, hard work, and love resulted in a miracle church.

Miracles happen every day. Expect yours!

Lord, teach us to use what we have to effect miracles. Amen.

The Miracle of Endurance

HAVE YOU EVER BEEN to the Bahamas and visited the straw market? There are rows and rows of stalls, each selling the same items at the same price. I really wonder how anyone earns any money. But, somehow almost everyone does. Some of the merchants have been in business for generations. They survive; they endure; and they accomplish the goals that they set.

One merchant has endured for thirty years. She has operated stall seventy-seven on Bay Street in Nassau day in and day out. She has managed to earn enough money to send her children to college in the United States. That is a miracle, a miracle of endurance.

One of her children graduated from Clark Atlanta University where I teach. I saw this student on a trip to Nassau; she was operating her mother's stall. She expressed appreciation for her mother's willingness to endure the close quarters, the weather, and the tourists in hopes of making life better for their family. Like me, she felt that it was a miracle.

Miracles happen every day. Expect yours!

Lord, thank You for those who are willing to endure. Teach us all to have patience and persistence as we seek to become better prepared to serve You. Amen.

The Miracle of Hope

JIM HOWARD WAS A VERY OUTGOING Atlanta city official. His daughter, Sheryl, was a student of mine. Sheryl told me her miracle of hope.

Her father had lung cancer, and each time he was admitted to the hospital for treatment, Sheryl felt that he would not come home. Nine times Jim was admitted to the hospital, and, miraculously, nine times he came home. And each time Sheryl was strengthened in her hope for his recovery. The hope that she had gained seemed to her to be a miracle.

It was this hope that helped Sheryl through the tenth and final time her father was admitted to the hospital. As she sat in the intensive care unit and watched the respirator do one hundred percent of her father's breathing, she knew that the father who had loved her and made sacrifices for his family and for others of his city existed no more. Her hope for his continued life in the earthly body that now caused him so much pain was converted to hope for his eternal salvation in a heavenly body no longer subject to pain. Sheryl was able to accept her father's death knowing that she would always remember and love him for all that he had meant to her in his earthly life. She had a new miracle of hope—hope that she would one day be united with him in one of the many rooms in the mansion above!

Miracles happen every day. Expect yours!

Lord, thank You for the miracle of hope and for our promised salvation. Amen.

The Miracle of No Name

WALLY AMOS LOVES TO COOK. In fact, he is known for being the inventor of the Famous Amos Chocolate Chip Cookies. Wally became rich selling his cookies, but he made some mistakes. He lost his cookie company, and he lost the right to use his name on any cookies that he might invent. Can you imagine losing the right to what seems to be yours only—your name?

Wally was not discouraged, for he knew that the same God who had given him the recipe for his Famous Amos Cookies would give him another recipe. He says, "God gives you as many second chances as you ask for." That very philosophy is the source of many miracles. How many of us bother to ask for a second chance? How many of us just give up?

But Wally did not give up. He asked for and got a second chance. Without a name, he developed Uncle No Name Cookies. He says that nobody buys the name and throws away the cookie. Any name or no name will do. All the consumer wants are the cookies. Wally feels that God helped him grow through adversity. He did not go through hardships; he *grew* through them. He experienced a miracle when he discovered that names are not important; results are.

Miracles happen every day. Expect yours!

Lord, we want to have good names, but we would rather be good people. Amen.

The Miracle of Running

ON NOVEMBER 12, 1994, she finished her race. She had been a fighter all of her life, and although brain cancer took her, she was victorious.

She was the twentieth of twenty-two children born to Blanche and Eddie Rudolph. When she was four years old, she was stricken with double pneumonia, scarlet fever, and polio. The doctors told her that she would never walk, and her mother thought that her child would surely die. But Wilma proved them all wrong. She had a strong spirit of determination, and she knew that she would not only walk but also run.

Her whole family helped her. They took turns massaging her little shriveled legs, and eventually she was able to walk with a brace. By the time she was nine years old, she walked without a brace. Her family kept working with her and telling her to expect her miracle, and in time, she learned to jump and run. Those little legs kept growing, and by the time she was a junior in high school, she was six feet tall.

Wilma's height, combined with her running and jumping skills, made her a basketball star. But basketball was not to be her sport of fame, for Wilma was noticed by Ed Temple, track coach at Tennessee State University. He trained her for the Olympic track team. There probably was no one more proud of her than he when, in 1960, she became the first American woman to win three Olympic gold medals in track and field.

The little girl who was told that she would never walk won Olympic gold as a runner. It was a miracle, and now she has run on to Glory!

Miracles happen every day. Expect yours!

Lord, keep us mindful that You are in charge. We may not walk with others, but we will run with You. Amen.

The Miracle of Faith

ALTHOUGH FAITH IS SOMEHOW INVOLVED in almost every miracle, it seems especially important to this one. Marci was three months pregnant with her first child. She had prayed in faith to become pregnant, and she had carefully followed all of the prenatal care her doctor had suggested; however, at her last visit, she had been informed that the child she carried was mentally challenged and abortion was an option she should consider. Somehow Marci did not believe the medical reports. The child for whom she had prayed could not be mentally challenged, but the doctor was certain.

Marci believed that abortion would be the coward's way out. It would testify to her lack of faith. She felt that God would make everything right. God could even change the results of the tests. The God she believed in had all power in His hands. Even if God did not change the bleak future of her child, she felt that any child God gave her was to be loved and nurtured. She would just have to find a way to care for a mentally challenged child.

Marci told the doctor that she would not consider abortion. She had decided to wait faithfully on God and the baby. Her doctor suggested classes on the care of mentally challenged children, for he wanted her to be fully prepared for the difficult job that awaited her. Marci took the classes, but she prayed that she would not need them.

The next six months passed slowly. The doctor never changed his diagnosis, and Marci never lost her faith. When it was finally time to deliver, Marci turned it over to God. She delivered a bright, healthy, normal boy. The doctor could not believe it, but Marci knew that her faith had been rewarded. It was a miracle!

Miracles happen every day. Expect yours!

Lord, give us faith that passes understanding. Help us to patiently wait for the miracles You've planned. Amen.

Conclusion

WHO'S TO SAY WHAT A MIRACLE IS? For some of us, it requires the parting of the waters or the burning bush that is not consumed or the instant restoration of a broken limb; for others, the safe birth of a healthy child or waking up in our right minds or contacting a loved one who had been missing from our lives would be miracles. Perhaps all of us are right, for whenever we are knowingly touched by God in such a way that our lives are changed for the better, we have experienced a miracle.

God knows that some of us need to see angels and some of us need to be shaken from our unbelief by typically impossible occurrences, while others of us can be moved by simple things. No matter how great or small, whether everyday or once in a lifetime, we all experience miracles. I am convinced that they really do happen every day for those who are expecting them. Are you expecting yours?